foundations of elementary education

J. MURRAY LEE

THE ALLYN AND BACON SERIES
FOUNDATIONS OF EDUCATION

FOUNDATIONS
OF
ELEMENTARY
EDUCATION

Foundations
of
Elementary
Education

by

J. Murray Lee

Department of Elementary Education
Southern Illinois University

Edited by

Myrtle F. Lee

Allyn and Bacon, Boston

PREFACE

This introduction to elementary education is written especially for those who are seriously planning to become elementary teachers.

It is designed to help one become familiar with what must be learned about the teaching profession and to help the prospective teacher decide whether he is uniquely suited to the work. Teaching is a job of first-ranking importance, not a tentative solution for the undecided.

Certain additional purposes have influenced the selection of the content. These are:

1. To help to realize that many changes are taking place in all phases of elementary education. Practically every chapter describes newer developments. Where vital questions concerning the developments have not been answered, such questions are raised. It is hoped that the reader will begin a questioning attitude which will continue into future courses and his teaching career.

2. To help to understand the importance of educational research, Chapter 1 introduces a few basic terms to help one read research. Chapters 4 and 6 present findings from research. Two of the other chapters [3 and 5] are based on the findings of research. Many unanswered questions are included throughout the book. It is hoped that this approach will result in a few more teachers being concerned with research findings now and in doing research in the future.

3. To encourage the reader to make the much-criticized abstract theory of education courses come alive through working with children and observing classes. Specific suggestions for observation and participation have been given in

the hope that concepts learned in class will become real in terms of behavior of boys and girls and procedures used by teachers.

4. To encourage one to be self-directive and seek wider experiences than can be had in the college classroom.

Needed competencies are pointed out, the values of liberal arts courses are stressed, and opportunities to become acquainted with materials are described where pertinent.

Such a treatment is not a compendium, but rather a selection distillation. It is hoped that it will give the prospective elementary teacher some idea of the depth of scholarship needed to be an elementary teacher.

In the usual Foundations of Education or Introduction to Education courses there are many students who are planning to become elementary school teachers. These students need to obtain insight and information regarding the unique problems of the elementary school, the nature of the elementary school child and the special requirements of his teachers, directions in contemporary development of curricula and organization, and the significant contributions of recent research in the field.

The volume is a condensed version of *Elementary Education, Today and Tomorrow* published by Allyn and Bacon, 1967. William Legge was most helpful in preparing bibliographies for that volume as was Judith Seiters. Mohammed Ali Bathee and Charles Mason made helpful suggestions on material to be omitted.

I owe a special debt of gratitude to my wife Myrtle for many a vivid and concise phrase and for her merciless editing of the manuscript.

J.M.L.

CONTENTS

Improving Your Own Learning

You are not alone, you know, if the day when you will actually face your first class as a fully accredited teacher seems incredibly remote and probably impossible to attain. So it did to the thousands upon thousands of elementary education majors who have preceded you—in 1967 there were 85,358 newly prepared elementary teachers and that figure none too great for the demand. They all began with motivations ranging from fuzzy inclination to firm commitment. Many who started the race did not finish, doubtless to the mutual advantage of themselves and the children.

Why do young people choose to be elementary school teachers? Some decide early that they want to work with children and have a backlog of experiences in youth work prior to college. Others are attracted by the idealistic aspects of service involved in teaching. Such motives are commendable but may wither when exposed to the realities of child behavior. More than sentiment was required even by Mr. Chips, the hero of James Hilton's novel, *Goodbye Mr. Chips*. Paradoxically, some unfocused drifters find purpose and direction when they begin to see what teaching is all about. Now and again some grossly misinformed idler enters the field because he has been told that teaching is an easy job. Hopefully he will depart as will the equally expendable reluctant recruits whose choice is based solely on family tradition. That teaching calls for participants, not spectators, is one of the first concepts a beginner must accept.

How about you? As you learn to analyze behavior in the courses which prepare you for teaching, your own growth will be enhanced by increasingly skillful self-appraisal. By the time you step into that first classroom you should know why you are there and what you want to do. Endless frustration awaits the timeserver whose principal skill in teaching is acuity in hearing the dismissal bell.

For contemporary graduates in elementary education commencement is literally only the beginning as schools change and expand to meet the kaleidoscopic world they serve. Opportunities for specialization and advancement are there for teachers who want to put forth the time and effort to attain them. Some areas of subject matter change so rapidly that the teacher must take frequent graduate courses to prevent premature superannuation. Teaching is for *dynamic* not reminiscent thinkers. The only verity that will not change is that there will always be children who will always need memorable teachers. You may be one of these teachers.

Presumably the class in which the reader is using this text is his first professional course. Vital preparation for becoming an elementary school teacher cannot be accomplished only by the academic exercises of listening to lectures, reading the assigned texts, and writing adequate but pedestrian term papers. It requires a great deal of energetic self-direction on the reader's part. He needs to observe and work with children; to observe and work in classrooms; to acquire a broad education; to read widely and selectively; to read research studies and other professional literature having significance for elementary education; to become acquainted with instructional materials used in the elementary schools such as text books, children's books, films, film strips, television programs, recordings and programmed materials; and to participate in student organizations on the campus relating to teaching, i.e., the state group of the Student National Education Association and the Association for Childhood Education.

Preparing to teach in the elementary school is a broadening experience. One needs to be a well informed citizen with a variety of interests as well as a competent professional person. Teaching is no sheltered retreat from the issues and life of the community.

OBTAINING A BROAD EDUCATION

Most college programs for the preparation of elementary school teachers require courses in the sciences, social sciences, behavioral sciences, language arts, art, music, and philosophy. All such courses contribute directly and indirectly to your competency as a teacher. In studying such courses be sure to understand the major generalizations, focal ideas, and methods of inquiry used in each field.

OBSERVING AND WORKING WITH CHILDREN

Observation of boys and girls of all ages is necessary if the concepts acquired in child development courses are to have meaning. Use emerging ideas as you go along the street, shop in a supermarket, eat in a restaurant, courageously attend a Saturday movie matinee, pass a playground, or dodge the children coming out of Sunday school. Little boys catapulting out of a Sunday school lesson on "love one another" and beating each other's heads with their Sunday school papers vividly portray the fact that "learning verbal concepts does not necessarily result in a change of behavior."

Observing the way different parents handle their children can be most revealing. Baby-sitting can be both a profitable and instructive experience. Serving as a leader in boys and girls groups, such as Scouts, Campfire Girls, or church groups, will make discipline less of a mystery in the classroom. Working as an advisor in summer camps of normal or handicapped children can also be most rewarding. Even serving as a waitress or busboy in a summer resort can give invaluable insights on the behavior of children and their parents.

OBSERVING AND WORKING IN THE CLASSROOM

Throughout this book are many specific suggestions for improving observation of classroom procedures. If the reader has regularly scheduled observations in connections with this course, these suggestions should be most helpful when related to what he sees.

Many observations can be done on one's own initiative. A good opportunity occurs during college vacations when schools in local communities are in session. It is important to remember, however, that certain courtesies and protocol are necessary. One always obtains permission from the principal before visiting a school. This requirement is not set up to discourage or exclude visitors but to protect children and teachers from undesirable intrusions. Once one has clarified his interest in visiting classes as a prospective teacher, he undoubtedly will be welcomed and will gain invaluable firsthand experiences. Since elementary school children look at a college student as contemporary with the principal, conduct and dress should be suitable.

Many institutions provide an opportunity to work in classrooms prior to student teaching. Take advantage of as many such opportunities as possible. Some institutions also help one arrange a September Experience, which may enable one to serve as a teacher aid in the nearest elementary school for a week or two at the opening of public schools, which usually begin prior to the college fall term. If the institution does not assist in making arrangements, a local school principal should be more than helpful.

READING WIDELY

Reading habits established in college tend to persist. Required course reading should not preclude other wide and varied reading, one aspect of which should be current news of concern. Reading selectively requires guidance in order to conserve precious time in a student's packed schedule—even sophisticated and experienced readers utilize reviews in such magazines as the *Saturday Review* or the book sections of major newspapers. The *Saturday Review* is particularly helpful to educators with its monthly Educational Supplement keyed to the most engrossing issues in the field.

In his professional courses the reader will be introduced to many professional books and periodicals. He should read more broadly than required and do some independent exploring. By the time he graduates he should be familiar with all major sources of educational materials.

The following description should help orient the reader. He should be sure at least to examine the materials in order to have a good idea of where to look for what he needs. A good orientation now will save hours and hours of lost motion later in his college career.

The Education Index

This index does for educational articles what the *Readers Guide to Periodical Literature* does for general articles. The Index can be found on the educational reference shelf. Articles are listed under major topics. Monthly issues are accumulated over several months, then into annual and two year volumes. The cover of the monthly issues indicates the numbers of the issues covered. Issue 1 is the September listing; issue 4 in December accumulates entries from issues 2, 3, and 4; issue 7 in March accumulates entries from 5, 6, and 7; issue 10 in June accumulates entries from issues 8, 9, and 10. Thus, if you wished to find in July all articles written on Federal Aid to Education during the previous year, you would look in issues 10, 7, 4, and 1.

The abbreviations used in the index are listed at the beginning of each issue. The entries are arranged as follows:

FEDERAL AID TO EDUCATION
American Youth Must Do the Impossible, H. H. Humphrey.
il J. Heath Phys. Ed. Rec. 34: 14-15 Je 63

The title of the article appears first and then the author; "il" indicates illustrations. The title of the periodical follows: *Journal of Health, Physical Education and Recreation*, Volume 34, pages 14–15 in the June 1963 issue.

The Children's Catalog indexes new books for children with a brief description and indicated grade level.

There are a large number of periodicals devoted to elementary education. The most important ones to be familiar with are:

General
> Childhood Education
> Education Digest
> Elementary School Journal
> Educational Leadership
> NEA Journal

One subject area
> Elementary English
> Social Education
> Arithmetic Teacher
> Reading Teacher
> Science Educator

Research
> Journal of Educational Research
> Journal of Experimental Education
> NEA Research Bulletin
> Review of Educational Research

In addition one should be familiar with Psychological Abstracts and Child Development.

Associations Publishing Valuable Yearbooks

Association for Supervision and Curriculum Development
National Council for the Social Studies
National Council for the Teachers of Mathematics
National Society for the Study of Education

Becoming Acquainted with Instructional Materials

Most institutions training elementary teachers have an instructional materials center where textbooks, children's books, programmed materials, recordings, and film strips are available. While descriptions in catalogues present some idea of content, there is no substitute for actually reading, listening to, or previewing these materials. This process should continue during one's entire teacher education program. The more familiar one is with materials and their use, the more effective a teacher he will become.

Reading Research

Educational research is increasing rapidly. In recent years financial grants have become increasingly available from foundations and federal sources such as the U.S. Office of Education and the National Science Foundation. States and local school districts are beginning to support research studies. The modern computer has made possible involved statistical analysis which previously would have been extremely difficult, time-consuming, and costly.

The modern teacher must be able to read and understand research reports. To evaluate research critically requires a knowledge of statistics and research design. It is possible, however, to learn to read research without understanding statistics and comprehend the problem the researcher studied and the findings he reports.

Most research articles are written following a similar format with approximately the same major headings. These are:

Statement of the Problem   Included is a brief statement of the problem to be studied and often a description of the population sampled, the instruments used in the investigation, and the procedure followed.

Previous investigations   Related investigations are often briefly summarized.

Findings   The statistical results are given in some detail.

Summary of Results   Usually the author will list the major conclusions from the study and discuss the implications of the results.[1]

Without a comprehensive background of statistics you can read and understand the sections on the statement of the problem, previous investigations, and the summary of results. One

---

[1]Research Division, National Education Association, Research Report 1964-R9, *Teacher Supply and Demand in Public Schools, 1964*, National Education Association (April, 1964), p. 7.

should skim the discussion of "findings" but not be discouraged if it is too technical to understand.

ORGANIZATION OF THE TEXT

The purpose of this text is to present an overview of some of the areas of scholarship which are most important to the prospective elementary teacher. Elementary schools are changing rapidly. Now is an exciting time to prepare to be an elementary school teacher. The sixties have seen greater changes in curriculum, organization for teaching, and designs for elementary school buildings than have taken place for the previous thirty or forty years.

Computers are rapidly expediting the tabulation and interpretation of research findings. Concern for the gifted and the economically deprived is motivating the development and testing of new patterns for working with these children. The 1965 elementary and secondary federal support programs have opened up new vistas and opportunities.

Most of the chapters in the book will give some idea of present knowledge or practice in the area under discussion. This background is by no means complete but is only an introduction to continued study in the area. In addition, there is some discussion of probable future developments full of challenge. We know some answers in elementary education, but there are many questions for which we need answers.

As a teacher the reader will find that each child is in some ways like every other child, but in many ways very different. It is these differences which will be stimulating throughout the teaching career. What works with one child will not necessarily work with another. Each group of children offers new problems demanding the best of one's ability to develop creative solutions.

Chapter 2 deals with the goals and purposes of elementary education. Chapters 3 and 4 discuss some of our present knowledge of children and some areas of exciting research where new insights will undoubtedly require new approaches and new programs.

Chapter 5 looks at the child as the learner and Chapter 6

at what the teacher does to facilitate learning. In both areas research and experimentation are furnishing profitable clues for action.

Chapter 7 deals with changes in the curriculum and organization of the school. These changes have many implications for basic preparation as a teacher. Changes which technology is bringing to the classroom are described in Chapter 8.

The modern elementary teacher has professional stature undreamed of in the days when hastily trained novices "kept school." Chapters 9 and 10 should help toward better understanding of the role of a professional individual. Understanding the bases of current and continuing educational controversies is a necessity. A teacher needs more than attitudes, often strongly influenced by his own judgments and values. His attitudes need to be based upon a sound foundation of knowledge and understanding in the area of controversy. He also needs to be articulate when discussing educational issues. Chapter 9 introduces you to some of the more important current controversies. Chapter 10, which treats teaching as a profession, examines the most important question—"Is elementary teaching the profession for me?"

SUMMARY

The kind of elementary school teacher the reader will be two, three, or four years from now, depends on how he uses his time in college. If he is passive, listens to lectures without much reaction, and does only the minimum assignment with languid effort, he will not be a very stimulating or competent teacher. If instead, however, he uses every opportunity to observe and work with children in and out of school situations, raises questions and attempts to find answers as he reads and listens to lectures, explores interesting problems and issues, relates material learned in his liberal arts classes to possible use in the elementary program, and evaluates and builds upon his strengths, he will be on the way to becoming a master teacher.

SUGGESTED READINGS

Abraham, Willard, *A Time for Teaching*, Harper and Row, Publishers, New York, 1964.

An excellent reference for beginning students in education. New innovations in teaching, individuality of children, and two chapters on controversial issues in education are most interesting and informative.

Association for Supervision and Curriculum Development, *The Elementary School We Need*, ASCD Commission on Elementary Curriculum, 1965.

Presents ideas on the type of elementary curriculum needed for the schools of today.

Bradfield, Luther E., *Teaching in Modern Elementary Schools*, Charles E. Merrill Books, Inc., Columbus, 1964.

Emphasis is on improving instruction in the various areas of the elementary school. Helpful references are provided.

Goodlad, John I. (ed.), *The Changing American School*, 65th Yearbook of the National Society for the Study of Education, Part II. University of Chicago Press, Chicago, 1966.

Chapter I discusses the changing role of the American teacher.

Harris, Chester W., (ed.), *Encyclopedia of Educational Research*, 3rd ed., The Macmillan Company, New York, 1960.

A valuable reference for workers in education. Recent research findings in all fields of education are provided.

National Education Association, *What Research Says to the Teacher*, Department of Classroom Teachers, American Educational Research Association Series.

Thirty pamphlets of varying nature, including spelling, listening, creativity and others, summarize important research findings in various areas of interest to educators.

Voeks, Virginia, *On Becoming an Educated Person*, W. B. Saunders Company, Philadelphia, 1964.

A book for those who are seeking to be educated. Includes information on the nature of an educated person, how to study, and personality handicaps that are disadvantageous to students.

2

Goals For The
Elementary School

•

We live today in a world which is so sophisticated in scientific knowledge that most of its people could be destroyed in a matter of hours. The traumas of such a world have naturally, but unfortunately, profoundly affected the elementary school. Controversy, often bitter, has surrounded the issues of what to teach and what the child should learn. Never has there been greater public interest in public education. This is an era in which the critical, but uninformed, often seemingly have favored access to the media of communication. It is an age when loudly proclaimed panaceas are seized upon as an easy answer.

Some of the ideas propounded are wisely based on the most significant changes that have taken place. Other voices are critical, disturbed, frightened and even petulant. They advocate a return to some halcyon but unidentified era of education when the world was serene and the happy child parroted prefabricated answers that disturbed neither teacher nor child with necessity for thought. Some of the most uninformed voices drown out people who speak with wisdom and authenticity.[1]

[1]J. Murray Lee and Dorris May Lee, *The Child and His Curriculum*, 3rd ed. (Appleton-Century-Crofts, New York, 1960), p. 3. Reproduced by permission of Appleton-Century-Crofts.

Teachers, today and tomorrow, need a strong foundation of basic educational values and research knowledge if the elementary education program is not to bend with every wind of uninformed opinion.

The children you teach will be adults in a future of many uncertainties, but there is one predictable factor—change: Scientists state that our knowledge is doubling every ten years. Included in our increase of knowledge is a marked rise in knowledge of how children grow, develop, and learn. Facing us always is the constant need to reevaluate our list of "imperatives" for a child's education.

The *modern* school has accepted a much broader set of objectives than did the *traditional* school. We know that the emotional and social problems of the child can prevent him from becoming an adequate learner. Reactionaries who say that the school needs to be concerned only with the intellectual development of the child are uninformed. We know that the world from 1975 to 2025 will be much different from the world of today. Objectives should evolve from what we know about the problems of the children we work with and our best estimate of the appreciations, values, and skills they will need in the world in which they will live. Objectives evolve from the needs of the society the children are to serve as well as the needs of the individual. The democratic values which we hold as a nation are a most important source.

GOALS OF NEWER PROGRAMS

During the 1950's a wave of educational concern swept the nation, accelerated by the launching of Sputnik by the Russians in 1957. Immediate attention was given to updating the elementary and secondary school curriculum. The unique feature of the many curriculum projects was the involvement of scholars from the various disciplines. These projects utilized new content and utilized in most cases the "discovery" method of learning.

Instructional objectives in these new programs tend to emphasize these purposes:

To develop concepts, main ideas, and generalizations identified by scholars as basic to understanding the structure of the disciplines.

To develop insight into processes of investigation used by scholars in the various disciplines.

To develop attitudes and appreciations related to the styles of thought and rational methods employed by scholars in the disciplines.

To develop independent study skills in order to promote lifelong learning.[2]

Teaching procedures which are used to implement programs in mathematics, science, social studies and health education stress inquiry and discovery. Michaelis has developed the following categories of objectives useful in viewing teaching strategies in all areas of the curriculum.

Problem solving: Objectives related to acquisition of understandings and development of requisite thinking and data-handling skills, as needed especially in areas of science, mathematics, social science, and health education.

Skill development: Objectives related to attainment of specific skills such as reading, use of native and foreign languages, mathematical computation, and athletic skills.

Creative expression: Objectives related to development of divergent expressive abilities in such areas as written and oral expression, visual arts, and music.

Analytical and appreciative response: Objectives related to development of evaluative criteria for use by the pupil as a "consumer" of art, music, literature, and other expressive forms.[3]

Recently Glen Heathers has provided a helpful way of thinking about goals. He states that "almost all of the commonly accepted basic educational aims can be grouped in three categories—content goals, process goals and personal-social goals."[4] Content goals have to do with learning about

[2]John U. Michaelis, Ruth H. Grossman, and Lloyd F. Scott, *New Designs for the Elementary Curriculum* (McGraw-Hill Book Company, New York, 1967), p. 38.

[3]*Ibid.*, p. 43.

[4]Judson T. Shaplin and Henry F. Olds, Jr., *Team Teaching* (Harper and Row, Publishers, New York, 1964), p. 348.

any field of knowledge. Heathers points out that the major content goals have to do with learning (1) terminology, (2) classification, (3) information, and (4) explanatory theory and technological applications of information and theory. As you view your college experience thus far, which of the content goals have been stressed?

Process goals have to do with those competencies needed in evaluating or using knowledge in a subject matter area. Heathers classifies them roughly into: (1) tool skills, (2) critical thinking, (3) creative thinking, (4) inquiry, (5) self-instruction, (6) self-evaluation, (7) interests, and (8) study habits. Which of these goals have been stressed in your education? Recent research to be discussed in Chapter 6 has given new insights into some of these processes.

Personal-social goals have to do with developing into a fully functioning person. Personal-social goals include (1) values—social, aesthetic and theoretical, (2) personality development—emotional security, positive concepts of self, self assertion, and etc., and (3) social behavior patterns—self control, cooperation and tolerance.[5]

Other approaches to developing objectives are the "persistent life situations" analyzed by Florence B. Stratemeyer and others[6], the "developmental talks of childhood" listed by Robert Havighurst[7], and the taxonomy of objectives in the cognitive[8] and affective[9] domain.

SUMMARY

Change is the one predictable element in the purposes and curriculum of the elementary school. The children you teach will be adults during the years between 1975 and 2025. Who

[5]Freely adapted from ibid., pp. 348–351.

[6]Florence B. Stratemeyer, H. R. Forkner, Margaret G. McKim, and A. Harry Passow, *Developing a Curriculum for Modern Living*, 2nd edition (Teachers College, Columbia University, New York, 1957).

[7]Robert J. Havighurst, *Human Development and Education* (David McKay Company, Inc., New York, 1953).

[8]Benjamin S. Bloom, *Taxonomy of Education Objectives, Handbook I: Cognitive Domain* (David McKay Company, Inc., New York, 1956).

[9]David Krathwohl, Benjamin S. Bloom and Bertram B. Masia, *Taxonomy of Educational Objectives, Handbook II: Affective Domain* (David McKay Company, Inc., New York, 1964).

can tell what specific knowledges, understandings, attitudes, appreciations, skills, and behaviors will be of most importance to them?

Specifically structured statements of goals or objectives are signposts, giving direction. The moment of teaching involves decisions as to content and ways of teaching to challenge and activate your particular children. Without goals decisions of one moment might be unrelated to the next.

Objectives also help the teacher maintain a balance in making decisions. One cannot dispense with the nurture of intellectual growth to create a delightful enclave where children are unfettered by any adult-designed demands. On the other hand recent observations of projects for gifted elementary school children indicate that over-emphasis on accomplishment is also a hazard to reasonably tension-free social and emotional development. Avoiding distortions and extremes, teachers must keep their programs in balance. A juggler keeping a variety of objects in the air is no more skillful than an excellent elementary school teacher who is not only a juggler but simultaneously the ringmaster for the show.

SUGGESTED READINGS

Goodlad, John I. (ed.), *The Changing American School*. 65th Yearbook of the National Society for the Study of Education, Part II, University of Chicago Press, Chicago, 1966.

> Chapter X includes a discussion of recent philosophy and normative premises for the schools.

Johnston, Bernard (ed.), *Issues in Education: An Anthology of Controversy*, Houghton Mifflin Company, Boston, 1964.

> Chapters 31 and 39 deal with the aims of education from a philosophical viewpoint.

Lindvall, C. M. (ed.), *Defining Educational Objectives*, University of Pittsburgh Press, Pittsburgh, 1964.

> Points out the importance of stating objectives for education specifically and making them behaviorally measurable. Shows examples.

Mager, Robert F., *Preparing Objectives for Programmed Instruction*, Fearon Publishers, Inc., San Francisco, 1961.

Stresses the importance of stating objectives behaviorally and meaningfully—with suggestions on how to do so.

Michaelis, John U., Ruth Grossman, and Lloyd F. Scott, *New Designs for the Elementary School Curriculum*, McGraw-Hill Book Company, New York, 1967.

Chapters 1 and 2 useful in determining objectives.

Morphet, Edgar L. and Charles O. Ryan, editors. *Designing Education for the Future, No. 1 Prospective Changes in Society by 1980, No. 2 Implications for Education of Prospective Changes in Society. No. 3 Planning and Effecting Needed Changes in Education*. Citation Press, New York, 1967.

These three volumes are essential in thinking about goals and planning education programs for the future.

National Education Association Project on Instruction, *Education in a Changing Society*, Washington, D.C., 1963.

Eight critical areas of improving instruction in schools are presented. The last chapter of the book (X) is concerned with tasks facing schools, in the light of the above areas.

Report of the President's Commission on National Goals: *Goals for Americans*, Prentice-Hall, Inc., Englewood Cliffs, 1960.

This report covers a range of topics which are of crucial importance to formulating objectives for education. Part one deals with goals at home; part two with goals abroad. Chapter three contains national goals for education.

3

The Child

Be warned. You will never meet The Child. He exists only in books about children. You will meet an infinite number of variations on the basic theme of The Child. Each child in any one of the classes you will meet in the days to come will have characteristics in common with his fellow classmates, but each will be a unique self. One will sidle apologetically into the classroom and its activities, conditioned by his experiences to expect little and to place his hope in drawing as little attention to himself as possible, while another will almost strut into the room, a happy, cherished hub of the privileged home from which he comes. Another will swagger and try your patience to its limits because in his harsh environment only the strong combative spirits survive.

What a job you will be called upon to do! You must encourage the diffident, challenge the over-confident and give him a goal to stretch toward, and calm the belligerent and lessen his conviction that the world rejects him. You must see the potential and utilize it in the ones who have handicaps that make simple tasks into mountainous difficulties. The Child —So many of him and only one of you to do so much for him, or so it may seem now.

You will not go into the job armed only with your own experiences as a child and random contacts with children along the way. By the time you enter the profession of teaching, you will have encountered a reassuring wealth of substantive evidence, the contribution of significant research in anthropology, sociology, biology, psychology, and education.

When parents take a child to a pediatrician, they expect the doctor to have an excellent background of training and to be informed on the latest scientific developments. When parents entrust the child to a teacher every day, should they expect less?

How can one find out about children? Future courses which the reader will take are one source. Courses in child development and educational psychology increase your insight into people. Biological courses aid in understanding growth processes, and socioloy and anthropology contribute to knowledge of the effects of culture and group living. Philosophy, art, music, literature, and religion illuminate the values motivating individuals and societies through the ages. The value of such courses to the prospective teacher can be increased by constantly asking, "What does this mean to me in dealing with children?"

EACH INDIVIDUAL IS UNIQUE

While studying child development, the reader will undoubtedly study physical development, intellectual development, emotional development, and social development as entities. When working with a child the teacher cannot separate him neatly into these compartments—neither his head nor his feelings can be separated from his mind. He has grown up in an environment which includes his home, his community, his culture, his friends, and his teachers. He is a product of all these factors.

Research tomorrow will illuminate present knowledge. A college education will not give final answers. When one becomes a teacher he will need to search continually for new ideas and their meanings in his work with boys and girls.

Questing and questioning are notable attributes of the college student who does more than complacently read only the assigned lessons and only the minimum of assignments. College affords tremendous opportunities for self-directed learning.

Man's Basic Drive is Toward Increasing One's Self-Realization

This drive involves the satisfaction of physical-intellectual-social-emotional needs of the individual. If this is so, why do individuals differ so in their behavior? Each person, child or adult, is attempting to meet these needs in the way he perceives them according to the environment and culture in which he lives. We expect differences between a Japanese child and an American child, between a child from the middle socio-economic class and one from the lower class. It is hard to understand differences between children of the same family. Such children differ in their abilities and in the way they perceive themselves, their family, and other phases of their environment.

Needs

In order to satisfy the basic drive of self-realization, certain needs must be satisfied. Needs exist in the physical, intellectual, emotional, and social phase of life. Various psychologists classify needs somewhat differently but a comparison of various listings show considerable agreement.

Physical needs include food, air, water, sunlight, activity, rest and sleep, elimination, and sexual activity. Intellectual needs include opportunities to seek and discover, solve problems, and exercise creativity. Emotional needs are centered in a feeling of personal worth such as self-confidence, some feelings of success, increasing self-direction, adventure, recognition, contact and harmony with reality, status with peers, acceptance with respect, sympathetic understanding, and love and affection. Social needs are closely related to emotional needs, i.e., the need to give affection, for confidence in others, for social contribution, to be of service to others, and for association in the "we-relationship."

SELF-CONCEPT

The self-concept is the way one perceives himself. Does the reader see himself as a competent student, one who gets along well with others? What areas of living does he see that he is a success in and in what areas is he not so good?

The way a child or adult sees himself affects the way he sees others and the way he sees his world. Research has shown that children with adequate self concepts use their potential more effectively than do those with poor self concepts.

Children come to school with concepts about themselves, their relations with other children and adults, and about tasks that they think they can do. While their concepts about school tasks are affected by the attitudes they bring to school, such concepts are further developed through their success or failure in school. Since verbal ability is well rewarded by school activities, the non-verbal child in the first grade can come to see himself as a failure in relation to school. What are the implications of this fact in planning kindergarten and first grade programs? What advantages would be offered by nursery schools or such programs as Project Headstart for the culturally different children whose linguistic ability is limited by their environment?

Research on the importance of the self-concept is continuing and increasing in scope. It is important for the prospective teacher to be well informed in this area.

PHYSICAL DEVELOPMENT[1]

An understanding of the general pattern of physical development is of the utmost importance to the teacher. Children all go through the same stages of physical development. They can vary, however, in their rate of development. Any class in the elementary school will have children who are at different stages of physical development. There is also a sex difference

[1]Freely adapted from J. Murray Lee and Dorris May Lee, *The Child and His Development* (Appleton-Century-Crofts, 1958), pp. 65–66. Reproduced by permission of Appleton-Century-Crofts.

in that in general girls mature physically earlier than boys. At age six the average difference is about one year, while at age twelve it is about two years.

Development is affected by heredity, maturation, and environment. As a result of improved physical care we see that this generation of children is in general taller and somewhat heavier than past generations. In studying the problems of an individual child, his physical growth and his physical condition must be given careful analysis. There is a high positive relationship between the amount of medical attention received by a child and the economic status of his parents. Economically deprived children have much fewer medical and dental examinations than do children from middle-class backgrounds. A study of data from Project Headstart during the summer of 1965 showed that the medical and dental examination which was given was a "first" for at least 70 per cent of the deprived children in one community.

Growth in height is very rapid in early childhood, slows down in middle childhood, increases during adolescence, and then gradually decreases until maximum height is reached. Early maturers begin their adolescent growth spurt as much as five years prior to some late maturers. It is easy to see why girls who begin their adolescent growth early and boys who begin it late have many worries about their growth problems. The girls are afraid of growing up to be too big and the boys of being puny. This deviation from the concept of their sex-ideal creates serious concerns.

In the first grade, physical differences are apparent in tasks involving muscular coordination, especially handwriting. Comparing a six-year-old boy and girl is somewhat comparable to comparing a boy six with a boy seven. One interesting way to observe physical differences is to watch a sixth-grade class square dancing with some of the girls towering over the boys.

Height, weight, physical proportions, and rate of maturation have considerable influence on personality and social development. The physical development of an individual affects his acceptance by others; this in turn affects his personality. Frequently a physical difficulty may result in seriously influencing the child's learning. This certainly is obvious in the case of the child with vision or hearing difficulties. While most teachers are quick to detect such difficulties, too many children are classified as "stupid" when either their vision or hearing needs attention. If a teacher is even in slight doubt about the problems of a child, he should first have the child's physical condition carefully checked.

Physical difficulties such as eczema, asthma, or glandular imbalance when appearing in early childhood sometimes are the results of emotional adjustments. Research is being done in this area and in a short period of time we may know a great deal more about the relationship between physical and emotional conditions. Certainly as a teacher you should never diagnose the cause of a physical symptom, but it is most important to be aware of the possibility that difficulties of adjustment can be responsible for certain physical difficulties.

Rest and physical activity are of great concern to the school. Young people need regular rest periods as well as periods of physical activity if they have been at their desks for a long time. It is not surprising that some children become restless with the amount of "just sitting" that goes on in most classrooms. Also, some children require more activity than others. With regard to physical needs, the teacher needs to help the child.

INTELLECTUAL DEVELOPMENT

Understanding intellectual development is of utmost importance to the teacher. From the moment of conception the individual begins to interact with his environment. This interaction, physical, mental, emotional, and social, continues as long as there is life. While mental abilities of children differ widely at birth, environment has a marked effect on the development of any natural talent. Studies of children reared in a lower socio-economic home show that these children enter school with a marked language deprivation.

For example, Bill is six years old and the oldest of three children. His mother works; the father has long since disappeared from the home. The family lives in two rooms. Bill is poorly dressed and has not played much with other children. When the mother gets home from work she is so tired that the words Bill hears most often are "shut up" and "don't." There are no magazines or books; he has never been out in the country or away more than a few blocks from his overcrowded street.

Contrast Bill's life with Henry's. Henry, also six years old, lives in a good middle class home with his father, mother, and older sister. The mother does not work and spends much pleasant time with Henry. Henry not only has many books of his own, but is permitted to enjoy his sister's. Both she and her mother often read to him. The family has taken several interesting trips during the summer. Henry has been on a farm and also has seen the beach.

Bill enters school with a stultifying handicap. Since most schools measure success in linguistic activities, his handicap increases. When given intelligence and achievement tests, of course Bill does poorly, and it is easy to see how he would come to be labeled a "slow" child. What kind of a child might Bill have been in an environment like Henry's? Should the public schools provide nursery and kindergarten experiences for the Bills of our nation? What kind of a primary program should Bill have? Such questions are not ones you can answer fully now but you should be able to make meaningful suggestions by the time you are ready to teach. As your background increases, one point of focus might be to apply consistently your new insights to such specific problems as meeting the needs of the Henrys and Bills.

INTERPRETING INTELLIGENCE TESTS

The intelligence quotient (IQ) is the usual method of interpreting intelligence test results. The IQ is obtained by dividing the mental age by the chronological age and multiplying by 100. ($IQ = \dfrac{MA}{CA} \times 100$). The mental age is obtained from the child's total score on an intelligence test by using the equivalent mental age from a table of norms in the test manual. (Many tests now provide tables which give the IQ's for each test score and chronological age.)

A child of 10 years 0 months (10–0) with a mental age of 8 years 0 months (8–0) would have an IQ of 80. What would be the IQ of one with a CA of 10–0 and an MA of 12–0?

What We Know About Intelligence

We know that

1. Children differ in intelligence. There will be a range from slow learners to fast learners in most classrooms in terms of verbal learning.

2. The most widely used intelligence tests measure the more convergent types of intelligence rather than divergent thinking.

3. When teachers use only a rating scale to identify gifted children, they may merely select high academic achievers, some of whom are not necessarily gifted. Such scales fail to identify the gifted child who is not an achiever in conventional classroom tasks.

4. The IQ is not constant. Studies have shown that a child's IQ can change.

5. While in general there is a relationship between intelligence and socio-

What Are the Implications for the Classroom

The teacher should

1. Adapt the work to these individual differences. The same level of work will not be suitable for all children.

2. Be alert to recognize signs in children of divergent thinking. Activities are needed to encourage divergent thinking.

3. Realize that the teachers' judgments have some degree of bias and use test data to supplement identification procedures. Tests of creativity should also be used when possible.

4. Avoid labeling children with a low IQ as "dumb." The proper learning and emotional environment may bring about changes.

5. Avoid estimating intelligence on the basis of parents' occupations or the

What We Know About Intelligence	What Are the Implications for the Classroom
economic level of parents, there is a wide range of intelligence at each level. A large number of the gifted come from the skilled laboring class.	child's appearance. Children with low IQ's from professional homes and high IQ's from laborer's homes may present problems in educational and vocational guidance.
6. Extremes of intelligence show differences in personality characteristics. While negative personality traits are related to lower intelligence it does *not* mean that lower intelligence is the cause.	6. Realize that the situation in which the child finds himself may produce such traits. The classroom situation for children of lower intelligence needs to be adjusted to their needs. They should not perceive themselves as failures.
7. The physically handicapped child is not necessarily mentally handicapped.	7. Avoid judging the mental ability of a child on the basis of a physical handicap such as cerebral palsy, epilepsy, or muscular dystrophy.
8. A child's self concept as to his ability to handle intellectual tasks affects his successful handling of such tasks.	8. Realize the importance of providing successful experiences for the child who sees himself as a failure.
9. The child is a seeking, curious being. He needs challenging, intellectually successful, and satisfying experiences. Creative activities are needed rather than complete involvement in prefabricated tasks.	9. Provide such experiences at "the growing edge" of each child. What is challenging to one child may produce anxiety in others. The teacher like the salesman must know "his territory." It is easy in the classroom to dull curiosity and creativity.

EMOTIONAL DEVELOPMENT

A child's life is more likely to be greatly affected by the way his emotions develop than by either his physical or mental development. We know that the way emotions evolve is more readily and extensively affected by environment than are either the physical or mental aspects of life.

Each child enters school with certain feelings about himself, his own adequacy, his parents, other adults, other children, and his world around him. As Bill entered school for the first time, how do you think he felt? How did Henry feel? How did the teacher appear to Bill and Henry? How do you think the feelings of each child affected his behavior in the new situation? It is going to be fairly easy to continue reinforcing Henry's feeling of adequacy. Why will it be difficult to change Bill's dislike of adults and of other children and fear of new situations?

Teachers need to understand the emotional needs of individuals, the ways people attempt to meet these needs, ways of working with children who use inadequate methods of meeting needs, the signs and behaviors of children who are emotionally disturbed, and what the teacher and other services of the school can do to help. What courses, readings, and experiences with children will help the prospective teacher gain this understanding?

The teachers need to understand that the feelings of the child are definitely related to the extent that emotional needs are fulfilled. The most important needs include a feeling of confidence in himself, love and affection, success, recognition, increasing self-direction, status with his peers, and acceptance with his peers. When the child perceives that the need in one area is not met, this area is most likely to become the center of his efforts to adjust to his world. Thus a child who does not feel he is loved may direct all his efforts and attention toward trying to get attention.

Experiences which meet the child's needs are constructive and pleasant. Those which hinder him in meeting his needs are destructive and unpleasant. Constructive experiences promote learning and understanding. The well adjusted child tends to perceive most situations favorably while the poorly adjusted child tends more often to perceive them unfavorably. Knowing this, a teacher finds it easier to understand why Bill reacts to some situations unfavorably when there seems to be no apparent reason for such a reaction.

Emotional responses tend with age to become more complex, interrelated, and combined. Thus such derived emotions become difficult to recognize and diagnose. Emotional responses also become attached to irrelevant objects and situations by association. Emotional reactions displayed in early childhood are very likely to continue in some form in later years. Bill will not "outgrow" his feelings. Situations must be provided to change his outlook on his world.[2]

As a teacher, you ask, "How can I learn to recognize the child with unusual emotional concerns?" There are a number of helps available to you, i.e., the ever-increasing number of questionnaires or "tests" which the child himself answers. These are self-report instruments and give you a cue to how the child sees himself, others, and his world. The California Test of Personality[3] is one frequently used. There are a number of unpublished ones of value for self-concept and anxiety. There are also a variety of rating scales for teachers to use. Such scales reflect the way the teacher sees the child. In many situations such instruments have value, but in others, such as estimating anxiety of a child, it has been shown that teachers cannot identify high-achieving children who are anxious.

Observation of the behaviors and reactions of children is still one of the best ways of detecting difficulties. Children tell us that they have problems if we are smart enough to understand what they say verbally or by their behavior.[4]

[2]*Ibid.*, adapted from Chapter V.

[3]Published by California Test Bureau.

[4]For further reading see J. Murray Lee and Dorris May Lee, *The Child and His Development* (Appleton-Century-Crofts, New York, 1958), Chapter 10, "Recognizing Behavior Cues," or Daniel A. Prescott, *The Child in the Educative Process* (McGraw-Hill Book Company, New York, 1957), Chapters V, VI, and VII.

SOCIAL DEVELOPMENT

Social development has to do with how we react to others and how they react to us. Visit a nursery school or kindergarten and try to locate the children who like others and are liked in return. Identify the "isolates," that is children who consistently stay by themselves. Social development as well as emotional is determined largely by the child's experiences.

Social needs are those which have to do with feelings about others. There is a need to give affection, to have confidence in others, to make contributions to the group and be of service to others, and for association in a "we-relationship." Such needs are closely related to our emotional needs. If a child's emotional needs are not met, difficulties will arise in relation to his social development.

Language provides a basic means of socialization. As the child learns to use symbols, he also learns conventional attitudes towards those things expressed by the symbols.

The child's interaction with others is most important in determining social development. Integrative interaction tends to promote development while domination of teacher, parent, or peers hinders development. Integrative interaction brings forth integrative behavior in others. Resistance to domination is an active attempt to maintain one's integrity. Teachers need careful study of resistant behavior to determine what is wrong in the child's environment.

The extent to which a child is accepted by others is apt to be fairly consistent through the years unless there is an effective attempt to bring about a change. Teachers have a great responsibility for working with the child who is an isolate. In observing in kindergarten or first grade, see if you can recognize one or two children who are isolates and who do not associate with others. Unless there is a real attempt to bring about a change in these children, they are very apt to continue as isolates throughout their school and adult life.[5]

The school has a responsibility beyond intellectual de-

[5]Lee and Lee, *op. cit.*, adapted from Chapter VI.

velopment. It must provide opportunities for good social inter-action. All interaction cannot be between teacher and pupil. There must be opportunity for pupil to pupil interaction in group work. Diagnosis of a child's difficulty in relating to others is even more important than diagnosing weaknesses in arith-metic.

UNDERSTANDING THE PERSONALITY OF THE CHILD

The same behavior observed in several children may be due to different causes. The same basic cause may show up in a variety of behaviors depending upon the children. Thus it is most difficult to trace the real cause of a given behavior.

We need to list all possible causes. Then we try to obtain information for each one to see if it might be the real cause or whether we can eliminate it from the list. When the teacher does this for a child, he will still probably have several possible causes. He should never jump to a quick conclusion and label the student lazy or dumb. One would not tolerate a doctor who jumped to superficial conclusions, and children deserve as much professional consideration.

One of the interesting things that very frequently occurs is that as the teacher begins to find out more about a child, he sees him differently and he begins to work with him differ-ently. As a result, the child begins to respond differently, and the reader wonders what has brought about the improvement.

In the discussion on the self-concept of the child it was pointed out that the way the child saw himself made a differ-ence in the way he saw his world. It is important to understand that:

The way we see others affects our perception of ourselves. The environment is different for each person for he sees it differently.

On the basis of the way we see situations, we set up hy-potheses or expectations for what will happen. These char-acteristic ways of perceiving account for consistency. Within limits then, understanding the ways a child sees situations enables us to predict his probable behavior.

The ability to tolerate ambiguity or uncertainty seems persistently to affect ways of perceiving.

Anxiety may build rigidity which is related to ways of perceiving.[6]

THE EXCEPTIONAL CHILD

Exceptional children are those children who deviate from the average child to such an extent that they need special attention. This attention varies from providing special classes with specially trained teachers to providing a wide variety of medical, psychological, educational, and rehabilitative services for them. Included in the group are mentally retarded children, the gifted, those with abnormalities, i.e., cardiac, and those with various handicaps, i.e., neurological, orthopedic, physiological, visual, social-emotional, educational, and cultural.

To the reader's classroom inevitably will come the exceptional child. Will he be able to recognize the problem the exceptional child presents? Will he know what special services are available to him in the community? It may be that the reader is especially interested in working with the handicapped. Such work requires special training in addition to that needed by the regular classroom teacher. At present the largest number of such special teachers are working with the mentally retarded, with speech handicaps as speech correctionists, with the physically handicapped, and as counselors. In general, with the exception of speech correctionists, the training programs for these special teachers recommend the usual preparation for the elementary school teacher, plus some experience in regular classrooms, plus the needed specialized training. Such teachers must meet the special certification requirements of their state.

The demands for teachers of exceptional children is rapidly on the increase. If you are interested in this area the references in the bibliography by Gallagher, Jordan and Kirk are excellent for you to begin your reading.

[6]*Ibid.*, adapted from Chapter VII.

SUMMARY

Understanding children is a necessity for teachers. Their variations in behavior and learning are continuous replenishment to all who work with them. A worker on an assembly line adds the same part to each passing identical product. In teaching, no product or part to be added is alike. The teacher needs to know what research says about children so he can better understand each individual.

You have been given only a thought-provoking insight into the basic needs of the child, the importance of the ways he sees himself, and his physical, intellectual, emotional, and social development. These preliminary insights need to be validated by much intensive academic study and reinforced by actual experience with boys and girls. At least some of the academic subject matter you will be teaching will remain relatively stable. Not so the children—no matter how many years you teach, you will never regard the unending variations on The Child as dull or predictable.

SUGGESTED READINGS

Bany, Mary A. and Lois V. Johnson, *Classroom Group Behavior: Group Dynamics in Education*. The Macmillan Company, New York, 1964.

This book examines group characteristics, factors influencing group behavior, the effect of the group upon individual behavior, and solutions and procedures for coping with realistic problems. Draws heavily upon research findings for its textual matter.

Bernard, Harold W., *Human Development in Western Culture*, Allyn and Bacon, Inc., Boston, 1962.

This book integrates anthropological and sociological aspects of human development. Chapter IV is concerned with social class and its implications for education.

Bloom, Benjamin S., *Stability and Change in Human Characteristics*, John Wiley and Sons, Inc., New York, 1966.

Includes implications for social and educational planning based on a comparison of the findings of major longitudinal studies of youngsters with other relevant research on human intelligence and achievement.

Doll, Ronald C. and Robert S. Fleming, (eds.), *Children Under Pressure*, Charles E. Merrill Books, Inc., Columbus, 1966.

A book of readings dealing with parental and school pressures on children and suggested remedies.

Gallagher, James J., *Teaching the Gifted Child*, Allyn and Bacon, Inc., Boston, 1964.

Chapters on working with gifted children in various subject areas are interesting and helpful. An extensive bibliography is provided.

Goodlad, John I. (ed.), *The Changing American School*, 65th Yearbook of the National Society for the Study of Education, Part II, University of Chicago Press, Chicago, 1966.

Chapter VIII deals with the nature of the individual, studies of perception, personality research, and research and learning.

Gordan, Ira J., *Human Development from Birth Through Adolescence*, Harper and Row, Publishers, New York, 1962.

An excellent basic text on child development with special emphasis on development of the self concept.

Jordan, Thomas E., *The Exceptional Child*. Charles E. Merrill Books, Inc., Columbus, 1962.

This book benefits the regular teacher by offering precise information about the causes, symptoms, and possible treatment of the whole series of problems combining to form the concept of the exceptional child. Extensive bibliographies are provided.

Kirk, Samuel A., *Educating Exceptional Children*. Houghton Mifflin Company, Boston, 1962.

This book discusses the various kinds of handicaps and their characteristics and offers suggestions on working with handicapped children. Bibliographies are provided for each section. Chapter I is an excellent overview of exceptional children.

Lane, Howard and Mary Beauchamp, *Understanding Human Development*, Prentice-Hall, Inc., Englewood Cliffs, 1959.

Sections on foundations of human behavior, growth from conception to young adulthood, and how children are studied will be helpful to elementary teachers.

Lee, J. Murray and Dorris May Lee, *The Child and His Development*. Appleton-Century-Crofts, New York, 1958.

Developed from standpoint of understanding the individual, understanding the development of the individual, ways of helping individuals learn, and ways of working with individuals and groups.

Torrence, E. Paul. *Constructive Behavior: Stress, Personality, Mental Health*. Wadsworth Publishing Company, Inc., Belmont, 1965.

A discussion of ways emotional factors disturb the mental functions of individuals.

4

New Insights On Children

Research is rapidly opening new and extremely important vistas concerning our knowledge of children. With the aid of the computer we can expect educational research to intensify in depth and penetration. The teacher of tomorrow will face a tremendous challenge to continue to keep informed. We are on a frontier of an explosion of educational knowledge.

This chapter deals with our expanding knowledge in two areas: understanding creativity in children and the education of culturally different children. The first area, creativity, represents the work of a variety of investigators but primarily that of E. Paul Torrance of the University of Georgia. The discussion of the culturally deprived reflects the thinking of educators who have worked in this area and also presents some of the current attempts at improvement.

CREATIVITY

The elementary school for many years has been concerned with providing creative experiences for children. This concern is not new. What is new is our increased knowledge of factors involved in creative thinking, the characteristics of creative children, and the personality patterns of creative adults.

J. P. Guilford, a psychologist at the University of Southern California, pointed out in 1950 the inadequacy of accounting for creative talent on the basis of high intelligence alone. From research on adults he identified the importance of the following factors in creativity:

1. Adaptive and spontaneous flexibility
2. Closure and intuition
3. Novel and original ideas
4. Sensitivity to problems
5. Fluency of ideas
6. Ability to see differences and similarities
7. Ability to rearrange and reorganize[1]

Interest in measuring creativity in children was stimulated by the work of Guilford, but Torrance has also been most productive. His most helpful volume for teachers is *Guiding Creative Talent*. After developing a number of tests to measure the creative aspects of thinking, he gave these tests and intelligence and achievement tests to a group of children. The top 20 per cent in intelligence were compared with the top 20 per cent in creativity. He then compared the two groups, eliminating the overlap which he said was "small." (Most studies find about thirty per cent common to both groups.) He found:

1. The intelligent group (I) was on the average 25 points higher in I.Q. than the highly creative group (C).
2. The I group was rated by their teachers as more desirable, better known or understood, more ambitious, and more hard working and studious.
3. Teachers in general considered the C group to have more "wild" ideas, especially the boys.
4. The children considered the C group to have both "good" ideas and "wild" ideas. The extent of recognizing "good" ideas seems to increase through the grades.
5. However, the actual achievement of the I and C groups as measured by achievement tests were equal. This means that the C group were achieving more in relation

[1] J. P. Guilford and others, "A Factor-Analytic Study of Creative Thinking, II, Administration of Tests and Analysis of Results," Vol. 8 (Psychological Laboratory, University of Southern California, Los Angeles, 1952), pp. 1–24.

to their intelligence than the I group, but the *teachers perceived the I group as doing best.*[2]

Do you think that the reason teachers saw the highly intelligent group in the most favorable light was their conformity to classroom routines and their unquestioning completion of learning tasks?

A study was made of the value systems of two comparable groups on the high school level by Getzels and Torrance.[3] They asked both groups of students to list the qualities making for adult success, to list the qualities that the students most envy and the qualities they believe teachers favor. The investigators found that for the high IQ groups the rank order correlation between the qualities the students felt made for adult success and the qualities that they desired was .81. For the highly creative group it was .10. This means that the high IQ groups desired to have the qualities that made for adult success because the .81 correlation is very high. The highly creative group did not desire the qualities which they felt made for success because the correlation of .10 is very low.

The correlations between the qualities the pupils desired and the qualities they believed teachers favor was .67 for the high IQ group. The comparable *r* for the highly creative group was —.25. This means results indicate that the high IQ group desired the same qualities they felt teachers favor, because the correlation of .67 indicates definite similarities between two sets of values. The highly creative group did not desire the qualities they believed teachers favor, because the correlation of —.25 indicates a somewhat dissimilar set of values. It is easy to understand why teachers preferred the high IQ group since the highly creative group had values different from the teachers. Other studies have shown that the highly creative group not only did not wish to emulate the teacher but that they did not wish to emulate their peers.

[2]E. Paul Torrance, *Guiding Creative Talent* (Prentice-Hall, Inc., Englewood Cliffs, 1962), 278 pp.
[3]J. W. Getzels and P. W. Jackson, "The Highly Intelligent and the Highly Creative Adolescent: A Summary of Some Research Findings," in C. W. Taylor, ed. *The Third (1959) University of Utah Research Conference on the Identification of Creative Scientific Talent* (University of Utah Press, Salt Lake City, 1959), pp. 46–57.

As a result of his numerous studies, Torrance summarizes the characteristics of creative children.

Creative children may not be well-rounded.
Creative children may diverge from sex norms.
Creative children prefer to learn on their own.
Creative children like to attempt difficult tasks.
Creative children may undertake dangerous tasks.
Creative children are searching for a purpose.
Creative children have different values.
Some creative children cannot stop working.
Creative children search for their uniqueness.
Creative children struggle with sanctions against divergency.
Creative children find that maintaining creativity may alienate friends.
Creative children suffer from psychological estrangement.[4]

Torrance's description of each of these characteristics provides fascinating insights into the thinking of creative children. As can be imagined from the list, they have many difficult problems to handle. Not being well-rounded, many have verbal abilities below their other abilities.

Perhaps the most inventive and imaginative child he has tested is a boy who has had unusual difficulty in learning to read, yet his store of information and his ability to use it imaginatively in solving problems and developing ideas is fantastic.[5]

These children struggle with pressures of parents, teachers, and peers to conform. Boys who are not interested in the usual patterns of boys' activities worry their parents that they will not be "he-men." Many of our school mores place a real penalty on being different. It is obvious from research that we as teachers have difficulty in understanding and recognizing the worth of these children because of our own psychological blocks.

Another interesting finding in studies by Torrance and other researchers is a drop in creativity in the fourth grade and another drop at the beginning of the seventh grade. Sev-

[4]Torrance, *op. cit.*, Chapter VI.
[5]*Ibid.*, p. 109.

eral explanations have been advanced for the fourth grade drop. One is that the drop is due to the desire to conform to peer group standards, a drive which becomes more marked at this age. Another is that the decrease may be a result of different teaching methods used in most primary and intermediate grades, thus creating new stresses.

Many of those pupils who experience this drop "sacrifice their creativity rather permanently, producing a serious loss of talent."[6] Some children recover and a few maintain their creative growth without the drop. Torrance found one fourth grade where a drop did not occur, because the teacher was a warm, accepting person relating unusually well to children. There was a wide variety of creative activities included in the program, and pupils were involved in planning many of their own learnings.

Observe if possible one or two third and fourth grade classes. What differences in teachers, methods, and learning activities are there?

Fully Functioning Individuals Compared with Creative Individuals

One of the major purposes of education is to develop individuals who can function as fully as possible. A most interesting comparison of the personality characteristics of fully functioning individuals with creative individuals is present in Table 4–1. In an unusual yearbook of the Association for Supervision and Curriculum Development (ASCD) entitled *Perceiving, Behaving, Becoming*, four psychologists, Earl Kelley, Carl R. Rogers, A. H. Maslow, and Arthur W. Combs, discuss the personality characteristics of fully functioning individuals. Many of the qualities they discussed are listed in the left hand column of Table 4–1.

The column on the right represents the personality characteristics of adult creative artists, scientists, engineers, and architects. D. W. MacKinnon of the University of California asked a large panel in each of the four areas to name the most creative individual in their area. The outstanding ones so

[6]*Ibid.*, p. 94.

named were studied intensively using tests and interviews. The items listed are the principal findings. The comparison was developed to show the *close relationship* which exists. The challenge to us as teachers is to provide learning situations and a school climate which will encourage the development of these qualities.

As you study the list, think back over your own experience. What experiences and teachers helped you in these areas; which ones do you feel hindered you?

Where are we? We need to identify the creative child as well as the highly intellectual ones. The present tests used by Torrance are suggestive but very time-consuming and hard to score. We need to experiment with curriculum and methods which will encourage divergent thinking. We, ourselves, need to venture and experiment more in developing learning experiences.

TABLE 4–1
SIMILARITIES OF

FULLY FUNCTIONING INDIVIDUALS*	CREATIVE INDIVIDUALS**
	1. High level of effective intelligence
2. Openness to experience, perceptual fields open to change and adjustment, considers all stimuli, rich and extensive field of perceptions, maximum of adaptability	2. Openness to experience, records and retains experience, fluent in scanning and selecting thoughts, wide range of information, flexibility with respect to means and goals
3. Thinks well of himself (thinks well of others, not fearful, can be wrong, accepting, doing what "feels right")	3. Relative lack of self defensiveness (absence of repression and suppression—freedom from crippling restraints)
4. Less disturbed by criticism, stable in midst of stress or strain	4. Not preoccupied with impressions of others

FULLY FUNCTIONING INDIVIDUALS	CREATIVE INDIVIDUALS
5. Not afraid of expressing feelings, negative aspects taken in stride	5. Admits psychological problems and speaks (general candor in self-description)
	6. Unhappiness in childhood (awareness to experience and inner life)
7. Discovering the structure of the experience instead of a performed structure	7. Perceiving rather than judging (not bound to presented stimuli; capable of occurring, not yet realized)
8. Standards will be unique	8. Independent (not conformists nor deliberate non-conformists)
9. Meaningful, more personal meanings	9. Interested in meanings and implicating (not small details or facts as such)
10. Exploring and discovering meaning	10. Cognitively flexible, verbally skillful
11. Involvement, accepts change, exciting, challenging	11. Delight with the unfinished and challenging (striving for solutions to more difficult problems)
	12. Thinking vs. feeling: artists operate primarily on the basis of feeling scientists and engineers on thinking architects are divided
	13. Realized his potential

*Freely adapted from Arthur Combs, Chairman, *Perceiving, Behaving, Becoming*, 1962 Yearbook (Association for Supervision and Curriculum Development, Washington, D.C., 1962), Chapter I–IV.

**Freely adapted from D. W. MacKinnon "What Makes a Person Creative?" *Saturday Review* (February 10, 1962).

CHILDREN FROM A CULTURALLY
DIFFERENT ENVIRONMENT

One child out of three comes to our elementary schools from homes which are "culturally different." "Different," "disadvantaged," "deprived," or "underprivileged"—call them what you will, their meaning all too often connotes a special challenge to the schools. These children may come from a crowded room in the heart of a big city or from a shack in a "pocket of poverty" in the country. What is the prognosis for their life's achievement? Will they inevitably be the "drop-outs," the unemployed, the receivers of public aid, the criminal? Is it possible that they may rise above their environment? Some of these children are Negroes; some come from Puerto Rico; and many are white children from both urban and rural areas. For some, their world is one of crowded dirty streets, gangs, large families crowded in one room, a mother-dominated family; for others, a dirty or wooden floor, the privy out back, hand-me-down clothes, a limited diet, playthings improvised from scraps.

In common are:

Limited conversation and vocabularies: "get out," "shut up," "no" and a number of other words best omitted

No books or reading matter in the "home"

Experience limited to their immediate neighborhood, usually the street

Usually a destructive aggressive behavior pattern—hardly one looked on with approval at school

Poor clothes, poor diet, physical defects uncorrected

Teachers who usually come from middle class homes with middle class value systems

Yet too often we expect these economically-deprived children to be as successful as middle class children in handling the same highly verbal learning experiences presented in materials dealing with experiences of middle class children.

Many of the schools which these children attend are in old buildings, poorly equipped, with few instructional aids and supplementary materials. Beginning teachers are often assigned there because the experienced teacher wants to teach in a "better" school.[7]

Does the expression that "every child deserves an equal opportunity" mean that each child should have the *same* curriculum and same program? We know that the same curriculum can be penalizing for some children while enriching life for others. One of the greatest educational challenges of our time is developing an educational program which will "light fires" in the culturally deprived. Encouraging beginnings have been initiated primarily in the big cities, i.e., in 1956 New York City began the "Higher Horizon" project in a junior high school and a senior high school. This project was a many-sided approach involving more counselors, smaller classes, more work with parents, remedial classes, and visits to concerts, plays, museums and other resources of the city. The results were promising: eligibility for college increased, achievement rose, and disciplinary problems diminished. New York's experiment has now spread to many other cities, and the elementary schools are beginning newer experimental programs. These vary but certain elements appear common:

> Attempts to involve and work with parents, varying from providing parents with classes and recreational facilities to discussions on how to motivate and help their children—in general such parents want their children to do better than they, themselves, have done, but they do not know how to help
>
> Nursery and kindergarten—increasing the children's vocabulary and experience, thus helping them get a more equal start
>
> Counseling services provided for the elementary schools to help teachers and to work with individual pupils
>
> More excursions and trips to broaden the experience background of these children

[7]For verification, read Patricia C. Sexton, *Education and Income* (The Viking Press, New York, 1961).

Increased provisions for audio-visual aids and supplementary materials

Providing after-school recreational programs, summer programs, and camping programs which involve both recreational and school learnings with individual tutoring

Development of new reading materials more appropriate to the children's cultural backgrounds

Inservice training programs to help teachers better understand these children and effective ways of working with them

Involvement of public and private agencies

Many of these efforts are experimental and on a small scale, but they are spreading. We need to move rapidly in developing methods for teaching social studies, science, and mathematics in "an intuitive, nonbookish way." Learning in these subjects need not depend on the child's ability to read.

Newer approaches to the teaching of reading need to be developed. The language experience approach to reading seems to be one of the most promising. The child's own vocabulary and sentence structure are used at first instead of that with which he is largely unfamiliar.

Work with families and more counseling seem essential. Elementary school counselors are definitely on the increase in well-to-do communities and are considered essential. There is a much greater need for such services in the schools of culturally deprived neighborhoods.

Nearly all of these efforts involve increased cost. Unfortunately, however, the communities needing such services most often have the lowest tax base. The Elementary and Secondary Education Act of 1965 (Public law 89–10) provided considerable support for schools in relation to the number of children coming from homes with less than a $2,000 income. It is expected that the increased research, experimentation, and new approaches encouraged by this financial assistance will make a tremendous difference in the education of these children.

While we have made excellent beginnings in large cities, little or nothing has been done in rural "pockets of poverty."

Teachers and administrators in these areas often have the poorest training in the state for salaries are low. School districts are small and impoverished. We need a great deal of experimentation with the assistance of the staffs of nearby universities to analyze the problems and to develop new approaches.

If you are especially interested in the possibilities of teaching these children, read all you can in the area. Arrange to tutor several children. Observe in classrooms which include these children. Listen to such children. Search your community for possibilities to be of service during the summer.

RESEARCH—A CONTINUING PROCESS

The discussion of creativity, and culturally different children, illustrates some educational concerns of today. Teachers have questioned; research has attempted to obtain some answer, often raising additional questions; and experimentation is underway to obtain further answers. There will be many questions you will want to have answered when you are teaching. Research may have already supplied an answer, and if so you should know how to find it. Other questions may only be answered by your own experimentation in your classroom.

SUMMARY

Knowledge in all fields is increasing at a very rapid rate. Until recently education and research was lagging behind the sciences. The federal government and foundations are increasingly supplying significant amounts available for research. Such funds and the use of computers is making it possible to accelerate the amount and significance of educational research. Local school systems are investing more time, effort, and money in research. The Project on Instruction of the National Education Association recommended that one per cent of each school district's budget be used for educational research.

This chapter has presented two areas as examples of current research illuminating our knowledge of children. It should be clear to the reader after reading these sections that such understandings should definitely influence the way we see and deal with children.

The next few years should see tremendous change in methods and materials used in the education of the economically deprived child. The Elementary and Secondary Education Act of 1965 (Public Law 89–10) will make this advance possible. It is also predicted that such an advance will greatly influence the education of all children.

SUGGESTED READINGS

Association for Supervision and Curriculum Development, *Perceiving, Behaving, Becoming*, 1962 Yearbook, Washington, D.C., 1962.

Discusses the fully functioning individual, as opposed to the one who just gets by. Self-growth, independence, and creative expression are included.

Bereiter, Carl and Siegfried Engelmann, *Teaching Disadvantaged Children in the Preschool*, Prentice-Hall, Inc., Englewood Cliffs, 1966.

Provides curriculum and methodology for teaching culturally disadvantaged pre-school children.

Bernstein, Abraham, *The Education of Urban Populations*, Random House, New York 1967, 416 pp.

Stresses the primacy of urban problems and insists on new direction in the training and recruitment of American teachers. To combat cultural deprivation, the author suggests specific methods that recognize and utilize minority backgrounds.

Coles, Robert, *Children of Crisis*, Little Brown and Company, Boston, 1967.

A must reading for understanding the problems of Negro children.

Corbin, Richard and Murial Crosby (eds.), *Language Programs for the Disadvantaged*, National Council of Teachers of English, Champaign, 1965.

An important work on teaching the disadvantaged which not only reports on already existing programs at all levels, but also presents many ideas and concepts useful to all who work in this area.

Cowles, Milly, (ed.), *Perspectives in the Education of Disadvantaged Children.* The World Publishing Company, Cleveland, 1967.

Fourteen experts discuss effects of poverty, children of poverty, and the implications for education.

Janowitz, Gayle, *Helping Hands: Volunteer Work in Education,* University of Chicago Press, Chicago, 1966.

Analyzes the community of slum children and their relationship with the world around them. Emphasizes the use of part-time volunteer help in programs for the disadvantaged.

Loretan, Joseph O. and Shelley Umans, *Teaching the Disadvantaged,* Teachers College Press, Teachers College, Columbia University, New York, 1966.

Based on the theory that disadvantaged children actually have intellectual capacities far greater than they are usually thought to have. Suggests approaches that can be used as guidelines in the formulation of programs for these children.

Passow, A. Harry (ed.), *Education in Depressed Areas,* Teachers College, Columbia University, New York, 1963.

Fifteen articles on problems faced by schools in depressed areas, learning and the disadvantaged child, and other topics.

Riessman, Frank, *The Culturally Deprived Child,* Harper and Row, Publishers, New York, 1962.

Challenges the public schools to adapt a program to include children who come from economically and intellectually poor homes. Offers concrete proposals for working more effectively with such children in the classroom.

Shaftel, Fannie R. and George Shaftel, *Role Playing for Social Values,* Prentice-Hall, Inc., Englewood Cliffs, 1967.

Stresses the tremendous importance of role playing for changing children. Includes 47 stories valuable for role playing.

Taba Hilda and Deborah Elkins, *Teaching Strategies for the Culturally Disadvantaged,* Rand McNally and Company, Chicago, 1966.

Excellent suggestions for working with sixth, seventh and eighth graders.

Torrance, E. Paul, *Constructive Behavior: Stress, Personality, and Mental Health,* Wadsworth Publishing Company, Inc., Belmont, 1965.

Discusses ways that emotional factors affect mental operations and ways that mental functioning affects emotional well-being and personality development.

Torrance, E. Paul, *Guiding Creative Talent*, Prentice-Hall, Inc., Englewood Cliffs, 1962.

Deals with many aspects of creativity and creative individuals—the importance and role of creative endeavor, identification of creative persons, working with them, and assessing creative thinking abilities.

Wann, Kenneth D., *et al.*, *Fostering Intellectual Development in Young Children*, Teachers College, Columbia University, New York, 1962.

Indicates how young children deal with information and offers suggestions on how to give children opportunities to move along faster and more efficiently in their learning development.

Woods, Margaret S., *Thinking, Feeling, Experiencing: Toward Realization of Full Potential*, Department of Elementary-Kindergarten-Nursery Education, National Education Association, Washington, D.C., 1962.

Emphasizes importance of awareness of activities that can help children in their total growth-potential and gives ideas which have been proved successful in helping children work toward full self-realization.

5

The Child Does The Learning

The child does the learning. This chapter should give you the prospective teacher an understanding of the way children learn and his role in helping them to learn.

Will you be a teacher who is so effective in guiding children's learning that new and challenging visitas open, that exploration goes on and on, that curiosity continues? Some teachers are so ineffective in this role that they blight interest and cause the child to develop a dislike for school. Even with such a teacher the child is learning something, but what he is learning is not likely to enhance his intellectual development.

Learning is a complex subject, but our knowledge is slowly being increased through research. Such questions as the following are of concern:

Can children learn to read at an earlier age?

What is the best method to use to help children learn to read?

What approaches and situations are most effective in helping the child from the culturally different environment to learn?

Can content be better organized to encourage discovery?

Can children learn better methods of inquiry?

What approaches and situations are most effective in encouraging divergent thinking?

What approaches and situations are most effective in improving the learning of gifted children?

What approaches and situations are effective in helping the child with emotional problems learn to cope with his environment?

Will different organizations of the elementary school help provide a better environment for learning?

How can we utilize the tools developed by our technological progress, i.e., television, language laboratories, teaching machines, tape recorders, and projection equipment of various kinds, for improvement of learning?

These are only a few questions to which teachers and researchers are seeking answers. For some of these questions we have partial answers and hunches but not complete answers. The purpose of this chapter is to furnish the reader with some insight into the learning process so he can visit elementary classrooms and begin to raise questions concerning the learning process. Without some such insight he will miss many of the factors in the interaction of the classroom which he should perceive.

AN OVERVIEW OF LEARNING

Learning is shown by a change in behavior as a result of experience. Prior to the sharpened observations which one receives from a course in child development, he probably would not pay much attention to a child who holds a book somewhat closer to his eyes than does the average child. If after such a course he immediately hypothesizes that such a child might have a vision problem and then check his health record to see what he can find out about him, learning has taken place on his part.

One helpful approach to understanding learning is described by Lee Cronbach. He points out that any act involves seven elements: the situation, personal characteristics of the learner, goal of the learner, interpretation of the situation, action, consequence (confirmation or contradiction), and reaction to thwarting.[1]

The *situation* usually offers several choices for action. When the reader is visiting a class and hears an assignment given, it appears superficially that all pupils are facing the same situation. Do they all look equally happy? Henry may see it as an exciting, challenging task while Bill may feel it is an impossible one. What other variations on attitude toward the teacher and assignment might have been perceived by an informed observer? Most situations have several possible choices of action. Many times the choice a pupil makes gives a clue to the way he saw the situation.

The *personal characteristics* of the learner limit the way he responds. Each learner is different. Each has a different self concept, different values, abilities, and wants and desires. Such differences will affect the way the child sees the situation and set his goals and pattern his responses. During the reader's classroom observation, he should select two pupils and note the similarities and differences in their personal characteristics.

The *goal* of the learner is his own and is usually a part of a series of multiple goals. The multiplicity and complexity of goals increase with age. Some goals are immediate, others long term. The teacher is involved more often in helping learners set up satisfying short-term goals. The child needs short-range goals which he can reach successfully. As the reader observes a class, to what extent does he feel that the teacher helps children set goals they could reach? Perhaps he feels that the teacher sets his goal and the pupils work toward it to receive praise or avoid punishment. Motivation is the process of helping and encouraging pupils to set desirable goals.

Interpreting the situation takes place before the child responds. He evaluates several possible responses and selects

[1]Lee J. Cronbach, *Educational Psychology*, 2nd ed. (Harcourt, Brace & World, Inc., New York, 1963), Chapter III.

what seems to him the most appropriate one. This is an area in which children can be helped. Often a child will think of one impulsive response and act without thinking through the consequences. Through participation in group discussions of problem situations children can improve in the technique of evaluating the probable consequences of several actions rather than just one.

The *action* or *response* is one element which appears to the child as best adapted to meeting his goal as he sees the situation. Often the child's response, if in error, gives a clue to the way he sees the situation. Helping him see the situation differently will probably result in an improved response. Bill, who sees the reading situation as a threat, may respond with silence. It is easy to understand that he feels the teacher's wrath is less threatening to him than the ridicule of the class.

A new situation is either perceived as a vague whole or as one clearly defined element. The first response of the child gives a clue as to the parts that need further clarification. The consequence of the action either confirms his interpretation or contradicts it. If it is confirmed or he thinks it is he will be apt to respond in a similar manner in the future.

Thwarting is the result of an unsatisfying consequence. The most desirable response to thwarting is to reinterpret and try a new response. The problem for the teacher occurs when undesirable responses such as the child's passively giving up because he feels his goals cannot be reached or becoming furious when pent up frustration takes place. In each case the child must be helped to reinterpret the situation. This is difficult with an angry child for strong emotion definitely narrows his perception. He sees things only one way, his way.

ROLE OF THE TEACHER

Let us reexamine the seven elements of the learning process in terms of the role of the teacher.

Certain phases of the *situation* are determined by the teacher in selecting the learning experiences of the class. As a teacher you need to know in great detail the best curriculum for the specific pupils you are teaching but you also need to be broadly informed on the curriculum of the elementary school. The curriculum will be discussed in Chapter 7. Marked changes are occurring in many of the subject fields, and every teacher must make modifications to meet the needs and abilities of his class.

Knowing the *personal characteristics* of twenty-five to thirty children is a demanding task. Without the background provided by courses in child development and the utilization of these principles in studying children, one would miss much of significance. The better one knows each child, the more effective a teacher he will be.

Helping children formulate acceptable *goals* and working for the achievement of these goals is a major task for the teacher. In most classrooms too little time is spent in helping children formulate goals. Too often, the teacher accepts the goals set forth in curriculum guides or textbooks and then spends time in providing learning experiences which he feels will help children achieve these goals. This practice comes from the fallacy that children learn what we teach. Children actually learn when they have a goal they are trying to reach.

Motivation is essentially "a process of helping the child *select some goals over others*. It is also concerned with helping the learner *perceive these accepted goals as being more desirable than others*."[2]

We have learned a great deal about goals of children that are important to the teacher. The goal of the child is individual and is usually a part of a whole series of complex and multiple goals. In various children different needs may lead to the selection of the same apparent goal and general pattern of response. The same need in various children may lead to the selection of different goals and/or to different responses.

Short-term goals can be utilized in helping the child realize long-term goals. Once an immediate goal has been reached there is some change in future goals. An activity which is not

[2]J. Murray Lee and Dorris May Lee, *The Child and His Curriculum*, 3rd ed. (Appleton-Century-Crofts, New York, 1960), p. 77. Reprinted by permission from Appleton-Century-Crofts.

related to an accepted goal of the child can be repeated endlessly without much desirable learning taking place.

The child needs to learn to set goals which are realistic for him. The level of aspirations set by the child who is successful in school is much more realistic than those set by the children who do poorly in school.

Teaching materials and methods make a real difference in the learner's acceptance of a goal and his sustained effort to reach the goal. The child does not select learning activities that are too easy unless he is under threat. Motivation is destroyed when the child is held to one task to the point of saturation. Persistence increases as the learner gets closer to reaching his goal. Co-operative setting of goals by the members of the class and the teacher provides for group and individual acceptance and understanding of the goals to be achieved.

Helping to *interpret the situation* is an area in which the teacher can be most effective. Most of our work in school deals with words. Words substitute for real experiences. Could you understand what an orange is if you had never seen or eaten one? Experiences are needed as a basis for understanding words. Many of the newer educational programs for the culturally-different children have recognized this principle and are increasing the actual experiences with reality by providing not only more field trips, but more simple sensory experiences such as tasting an orange and smelling a flower.

The newer approaches in mathematics utilize the principle in problem solving. As you examine Figure 5–1 notice the progression from reality materials to exploratory materials to pictorial materials and finally to symbolic materials.

Too often as teachers we are apt to move fairly directly to the symbols without spending sufficient time on reality and exploratory materials to form a basis for understanding. This is why as a prospective teacher you need to spend as much time as possible observing elementary classes and children in a variety of situations. These experiences are your reality materials, animate and often baffling.

Another area of interpreting the situation relates to the feelings of the child as he views the situation. If he feels it is

FIGURE 5–1
LEVELS OF LEARNING AND RELATED
INSTRUCTIONAL MATERIALS
STEPS IN LEARNING NUMBER*
(*Start reading from the bottom up*)

LEARNING	PROBLEM SOLVING	INSTRUCTIONAL MATERIALS
IV. Systematic Generalization	IV. Accepting of Results and Acting on Them	IV. SYMBOLIC MATERIALS experiences with visual and verbal symbols, textbooks, etc.
III. Verbalization or Symbolization	III. Testing of Results Obtained	III. PICTORIAL MATERIALS experiences with flat pictures motion pictures, diagrams, charts, graphs, etc.
II. Experimentation and Discovery	II. (b) Pursuing Plan of Action to Tentative Results (a) Considering Relationships and Preparing a Plan of Action	II. EXPLORATORY MATERIALS experiences with "laboratory-type" objects that can be handled, felt, and manipulated
I. Readiness	I. Sensing, Accepting, and Defining a Problem	I. REALITY MATERIALS first-hand experiences with real objects

*Illinois Curriculum Program, *Thinking in the Language of Mathematics* State Department of Public Instruction, (Springfield, 1959), p. 104.

threatening or too difficult, the range of his possible responses will be limited. If previous experience with comparable situations has resulted in ridicule or condemnation from his teacher or parents, his response will probably be ineffective.

The child who has a poor concept of his ability to do school work and the child who is highly anxious need to have clearly defined learning tasks which they can successfully handle. As they achieve success, tasks can be increasingly more difficult and somewhat less rigidly defined. It is a slow process, however, to develop feelings of competency and adequacy.

The *action* or *response* of the child supplies the clue to the way he saw the situation. Here again the teacher needs to avoid quick conclusions and to develop a series of hypotheses as to the interpretation of the response.

Teachers must strive for maturity and objectivity beyond the ordinary range of swift human reaction. The teacher will know that he is approaching this kind of behavior when his emphasis consistently shifts from *what* the child did to *why* he saw the situation as he did. Knowing the *why* usually reveals motivations making sense to him if not to the teacher. (Often the teacher will despair of ever being able to project himself into the no-adult land of children's reasoning!)

A classic illustration of a teacher jumping to conclusions was the case of a fourth-grade teacher. She brought a child's paper into the fifth-grade teacher and said, "Robert doesn't know a thing about subtraction. He missed all these problems. His third grade teacher didn't teach him a thing." A quick look at the paper showed that all the problems involved zero. His only mistakes were in handling the zero. He knew his other combinations. The zero combinations in that school were customarily taught in the fourth grade. What sleuthing should the teacher have done before magnifying the mole hill?

In some situations the diagnosis of the wrong response is fairly simple, in others much more difficult. It is usually more difficult if the child's feelings are involved. As you observe children in classes try to apply the *why* not the *what* test to their responses.

The *consequence* element is another important area for teacher action. We know that immediate reinforcement of a successful response strengthens the response. This is the major principle underlying the construction of programmed learning materials. The child finds out immediately whether he is right or wrong. If wrong he sees the correct response. This immediate response is of most importance to the child who is unsure of his ability. Imagine doing ten problems in arithmetic and being doubtful if you are getting any correct answers.

As the teacher observes in a classroom he should put himself in place of each child and imagine how he would feel to each response the teacher makes to the child. As you study educational psychology, find out about the effect of praise and blame on various personality types. This is an area in which there are excellent research findings.

Thwarting is no special problem for the well-adjusted capable child. There is no great feeling generated. He feels he can succeed so he tries a new response. With the unsuccessful, poorly adjusted child there is likely to be so much feeling that he cannot imagine another response and is thus blocked. It is with these insecure children that the teacher will have to give most of his effort during this element of the learning process. The teacher must remain calm, make the child feel he can succeed, and help him to reinterpret the situation and try again. If after trying, the goal seems too difficult for the child to attain, the teacher can help the child set a new goal which he can reach. Always the teacher must avoid emotional responses which the child feels are condemning him as a person.

This discussion has presented a brief but rather simplified characterization of the role of the teacher in the learning process. It should furnish an idea of a beginning basis for observing teachers and analyzing what they are doing.

LEARNINGS IN THE CLASSROOM

What kinds of learnings are developed in the elementary school? The reader's first answer will probably be to list the subjects usually taught. Children need facts, of course, but not primarily for the mere accumulation of minutiae involved in fact-gathering. Facts become important as the basic building materials for generalizing, for solving problems, for thinking creatively, and for developing attitudes and values. Fact-finding, when skillfully directed, is a most important means of developing a wide spectrum of skills and is involved to varying degrees in all areas of subject matter. While the development of skills in putting facts to work may be inescapably obvious in such areas as mathematics and science, learning of music, art, and games is not accomplished either without factual information upon which performance is based.

As an elementary school teacher working with children of all ages the reader is concerned with developing:

Concepts, understandings, principles, and generalizations

Problem solving, critical thinking, scientific thinking, and creative thinking

Attitudes and appreciations

Moral and spiritual values

Skills

Most of the subject areas emphasize to some extent objectives involving all of these areas of learning. Research has made significant contributions about each of these areas and is adding new discoveries each year. Educational psychology courses should give you an understanding of how to use in your classroom what is now known. When one is teaching he needs, as does a physician, to continue a program of current professional reading.

The reader should not expect his professional courses in education to provide him with "rule of thumb" answers to every problem that arises in the classroom. Rather, his professional knowledge will give him a basis for more effective means of analyzing the situation and seeing the elements involved including differences in children. As a result of his analysis he then develops a teaching strategy most appropriate to the goal he wishes to reach, the situation, the materials he needs and the differences in the children.

Newer curriculum materials have encouraged learning approaches to encourage discovery, inquiry, and creativity. At the same time other materials such as programmed learning programs utilize reinforcement theories.

SUMMARY

Unless the reader has wandered into the teaching profession by mistake, he wants very much to be a teacher that most children will remember as an outstanding influence in their lives. His ability to create an incandescent joy of learning for children depends upon his understanding of the way they learn. Children are curious, questioning creatures until their spontaneity is extinguished by dreary make-work tasks that presumably are designed to stifle rather than to stimulate.

One way of looking at the learning process has been briefly described. Some suggestions have shown the role of the teacher in dealing with the seven elements of the learning process as defined by Cronbach.

In a few years the assumptions of this chapter may seem naive and a matter of historical curiosity. New processes for gathering data will make possible nationwide studies that previously would have required an impossible output of time and personnel. The life sciences (biology, bio-physics, bio-chemistry, microbiology) are revealing hitherto unknown and often unsuspected relationships between the physical and intellectual aspects of man. Incredibly accurate means of observing prenatal development may, among other contributions, reduce the causes of brain injury and retardation. Long-term studies of child growth and development now in process will have yielded their contributions.

Who knows? Perhaps the reader will do a research study that will become an indispensable part of future knowledge about learning. It is possible, but at this point probably somewhat visionary.

SUGGESTED READINGS

Association for Supervision and Curriculum Development, *Learning and Mental Health in the School*, Association for Supervision and Curriculum Development, 1966.

A good treatment of mental health and its relationship to the learning process, including ideas and concepts to guide educational practice and planning.

Bugelski, B. R., *The Psychology of Learning Applied to Teaching*. The Bobbs-Merrill Company, Inc., New York, 1964.

Discusses learning theories from standpoint of value to the teacher. Fifty-eight psychological principles for education are summarized in listed form.

Cronbach, Lee J., *Educational Psychology*, 2nd ed., Harcourt, Brace & World, Inc., New York, 1963.

Directed toward application of psychological principles to the learning situation. Considers variables influencing learning. A helpful bibliography is included.

Garrison, Karl C., *et al.*, *Educational Psychology*, 2nd ed. Appleton-Century-Crofts, New York, 1964.

Part Three is concerned with learning and the educative process, and Part Five is concerned with guiding the child. This book can be read with ease.

Joyce, Bruce R. and Berj Harootunian. *The Structure of Teaching*. Science Research Associates, Chicago, 1967.

Extremely valuable for better understanding the role of the teacher in the teaching-learning process.

McCandless, Boyd R., *Children and Adolescents*, Holt, Rinehart and Winston, Inc., New York, 1963.

Chapters four and five are concerned with learning from a child development point of view.

Travers, Robert M. W., *Essentials of Learning: An Overview for Students of Education*. The Macmillan Company, New York, 1963.

Contains implications of research and theory for teaching. A list of 64 educational psychology principles is found in The Epilogue.

6

Improving The Teaching-Learning Process

Teachers have been working for years in attempts to improve children's learning and have tried out new ways of teaching that they hoped would be more effective. This quest will continue as long as there are teachers concerned with constructive change. Gradually our knowledge accumulates, with changes in practice lagging behind.

Current approaches are concerned with two areas:

What does the teacher do in the classroom and how can he best direct the learning process? Essentially this approach is an analysis and improvement of the teaching process.

How can the processes of learning be better developed? Can techniques involving discovery, inquiry, divergent thinking, and concept formation be more effectively utilized by children as they learn?

Actually these two approaches are closely related, since what the teacher does certainly has some influence on learning. They have been separated here to indicate that current research seems to be distinguishing between two approaches to the total problem of improving the teaching-learning process.

Recently there has been an increase in studies of what teachers actually do in the classroom. Such studies are difficult and time consuming because one or more observers must watch one teacher over a period of time, recording all types of behavior on a predetermined list of behaviors or categories. If, in addition, pupils' responses to teacher behavior is included, the process becomes very complicated.

The pattern of continuing instruction is a highly complex one. Throughout this volume certain suggestions have been made on what to observe in the classrooms one visits. If the reader analyzes these suggestions, they will direct his attention to only one factor at a time, instead of the total pattern of reaction. When the trained observer has difficulty with the pattern, such an analysis is practically impossible for the beginning student.

The first study involving teachers' classroom behavior was conducted before 1914. It evolved from dissatisfactions over ways used by supervisors in evaluating teachers. The attempt was directed toward making supervisors' judgments more valid. Current research in this area seems motivated primarily by two purposes. One is basically the same as the above, to determine if supervisors can distinguish between good and poor teachers. Some of the present research is an attempt to provide a basis for merit rating in order to determine salary increases for the best teachers. These results will be discussed in Chapter 9. The second purpose is to try to develop a theory of instruction. The major value of such a theory would be the improvement of preservice and in-service training of teachers.

Classroom Climate

Social psychologists began to develop an interest in interactions between pupil and pupil, and pupil and teacher as early as 1929. The classic studies conducted in public school classrooms are those directed by Harold H. Anderson of Michigan State University. He developed an observation schedule to record whether the contact of the teacher with the child was "integrative" or "dominative." In addition, he included a technique to evaluate pupil behavior so he could determine how the teacher's reactions affected the child.

His studies brought out clearly that integrative behavior on the part of the teacher begets cooperation from the pupil and increases the child's emotional health and development. The children felt a greater sense of personal worth and increased their socially contributive relations with others. On the other hand domination by the teacher increased resistance and decreased emotional health and development.[1] The terms "integrative" and "dominative" are closely related to the behavior implied in studies of Kurt Lewin in which he used the terms "democratic" and "autocratic." He found the same pattern of reactions in out-of-school situations.

Classroom Observations

There have been numerous observation schedules developed to measure as much as possible of what goes on in a class.

F. G. Cornell and others were interested in measuring differences in classrooms as a means of characterizing differences in school systems. Their schedule was divided into seven dimensions:

A. Differentiation—extent to which provision is made for individual differences

B. Social Organization—group structure and patterns of interaction among individuals

C. Initiative—extent to which pupils control the learning situation

D. Content—source and organization of the content of learning

E. Variety—extent to which a variety of techniques is used

F. Competency—differences in technical performance of teachers in a few selected behaviors

[1] This study and other studies to be mentioned in this section are briefly described in N. L. Gage, ed., *Handbook of Research on Teaching* (Rand McNally & Company, Chicago, 1963), Chapter VI.

G. and H. Classroom climate—behavior of teacher (G)—
   behavior of students (H)[2]

Items under A through E were checked once every five
minutes and items under F, G, and H were checked at the
end if observed once or more during the visit. When two observers used the scale at the same time, there was generally
close agreement.

Other interesting studies are those of Marie Hughes done
in elementary classrooms and those of Ned Flanders done in
secondary classrooms. Marie Hughes used seven categories of
behavior, finding wide differences in teachers' behavior patterns. She found also that there was a large element of emotion
involved in the response of the teacher to the child. One might
hypothesize that, for the slow learner, programmed learning
might be valuable, because there would be no emotional response of the teacher to the child's performance. One unique
finding was that teachers' behavior patterns are stable, varying
little from one observation to another. Other investigators using
comparable schedules found that teachers' behavior varied from
observation to observation.

Dr. Hughes classified teacher behavior in seven categories.
As a result of her study she feels that the following range of
percentages in each of the seven behavior categories produces
the optimum interaction for learning in the elementary school.

Controlling Functions	20–40 per cent
Imposition	1– 3 per cent
Facilitating	5–15 per cent
Content Development	20–40 per cent
Personal Response	8–20 per cent
Positive Affectivity	10–20 per cent
Negative Affectivity	3–10 per cent

Ned Flanders used ten categories of behavior, seven dealing with teachers' behavior, two with student responses, and
one when silence or confusion occurred. A recording of a cate-
gory was made every three seconds. The results were plotted

[2]F. G. Cornell, C. M. Lindvall and J. L. Saupe, *An Exploratory Measurement of Individualities of Schools and Classrooms* (Bureau of Educational
Research, University of Illinois, Urbana, 1952).

on a two way matrix using successive numbers as pairs. For instance, if 7, 8, 1, 4 occurred, 7 and 8 would be plotted, then 8 and 1, and 1 and 4. The categories and the interpretation of some of the areas are given in Figure 6–1.

The data can be tabulated on the matrix by use of computers. Flanders has had excellent results in working with teachers who wanted to change their behavior pattern by sampling their behavior from time to time.

The use of tape recorders, televised tapes, and computers make it feasible to do this type of research. Some teacher training institutions are experimenting with recording the performance of student teachers by television tape and playing it back for the student supervisor to analyze.

FIGURE 6–1
FLANDERS MATRIX WITH AREAS OF PARTICULAR INTEREST IDENTIFIED (ADAPTED FROM FLANDERS, 1960)*

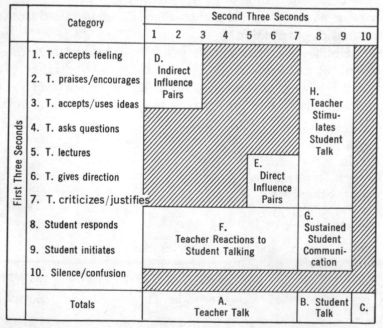

*Gage, op. cit., p. 273.

What is the future of such research? It may be that we can identify patterns of teacher behavior that result in optimum growth of pupils. Marie Hughes' study suggests possible patterns. We should be able to improve the preservice and in-service training of teachers and ultimately we may be able to develop an effective theory of instruction.

IMPROVING LEARNING

A variety of approaches is being used. The newer mathematics programs stress *discovery* as a basic approach to the learning of elementary children. The discussion of creativity in Chapter 4 stressed the importance of developing divergent thinking. There are two important additional approaches currently in experimentation—one on inquiry by Richard Suchman and the other on concept development by Hilda Taba.

Inquiry Training

Richard Suchman developed a number of demonstrations involving cause and effect on film in the area of physics. After viewing, the children then ask the teacher questions that can be answered by "yes" or "no." The purpose is to help them verify data in order to formulate hypotheses of cause and effect. The teacher's purpose is to verify answers, not to give leads. In a way it is a modification of the "How Come?" game in which a situation "with a twist" but with a logical solution is presented and questions are asked about it. "What's My Line?," the popular television program, was another variation of the same idea.

Suchman suggests that there are three steps of inquiry that pupils should follow. The first step is *episode analysis*, involving verification of facts observed in the film. The second is *determination* of relevance, involving identification of the conditions necessary for the experiment. The final stage, *induction of relational constructs*, is a generalization to be made from the experiment.

An examination of a film using a bimetallic strip may make the process clearer. The experiment is shown in Figure 6–2.

FIGURE 6–2
SUCHMAN'S FILM NO. 18: "BIMETALLIC STRIP"

Why does the blade bend and then straighten out?

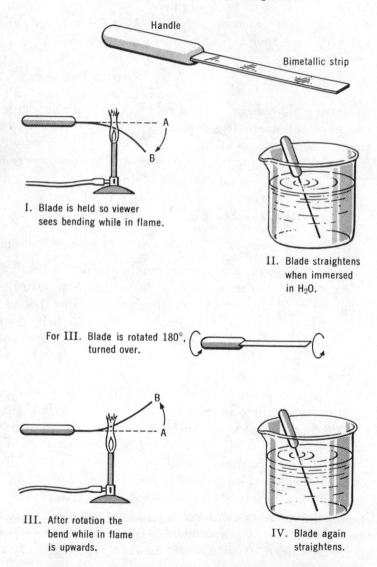

Handle

Bimetallic strip

I. Blade is held so viewer sees bending while in flame.

II. Blade straightens when immersed in H_2O.

For III. Blade is rotated 180°, turned over.

III. After rotation the bend while in flame is upwards.

IV. Blade again straightens.

James J. Gallagher. *Teaching the Gifted Child* (Allyn and Bacon, Boston, 1964), p. 219.

The first step, episode analysis, is shown in the following exchange. Steve is trying to be sure he has identified what he has seen.

Steve: Was this plain water in the tank?
Examiner: Yes.
Steve: Was this a special kind of a flame?
Examiner: No.
Steve: If you had used a wood flame would it work?
Examiner: Yes.
Steve: Was the blade hot when the film was going on?
Examiner: When it was being heated, certainly.
Steve: Did it melt?
Examiner: No.

The second stage, determination of relevance, suggesting changes in the situation is continued by Steve.

Steve: If this had been left to set for five days would it work?
Examiner: Yes.
Steve: Could this have been made—was this made any different way than any other knife you would think it would be like?
Examiner: Yes.
Steve: Did that have any effect on it?
Examiner: Surely.
Steve: Was there some chemical in the metal that did it?
Examiner: No.[3]

The mental processes of the child probably do not follow these three stages. He is likely to be searching for a hypothesis which he thinks might work, and he then follows through on it. This point can be seen in Steve's last series of questions. The questions asked by the children can reveal their perceptions of the situation. Helping them change their perceptions may lead to insight. Following the procedures recommended by Suchman, the teacher only verifies or denies the correctness of the perception. In other learning situations the teacher

[3]The dialogues are taken from James J. Gallagher, *Teaching the Gifted Child* (Allyn and Bacon, Inc., Boston, 1964), pp. 218, 220, and 221.

might ask questions that will help them see the situation differently.

There are many situations in the classroom in which such a procedure could be profitably utilized and the training would be significant. Certainly the regular panelists on "What's My Line" seemed to use better approaches than did the infrequent guest panelist.

The process suggested here is closely related to the suggestions made in Chapter 3 which relate to better understanding of child behavior. The reader should formulate as many hypotheses as possible concerning the reason for the behavior. He should accumulate as much information as he can that would lead to the acceptance or rejection of the hypothesis and continue with the process until he seems to have some verified hypotheses. In such a situation there is no teacher to tell him whether he is right or wrong.

Improvement of Thought Process

Hilda Taba's research dealt with the improvement of thought processes in the social studies in grades three to six. She worked with 20 teachers and 481 children in Contra Costa, California, where she was interested in whether training could make it possible to develop logical thought operations at an earlier age. She worked with teachers on improving the ability of children in three clusters of thought processes, namely,

I. Grouping, classifying, or labeling informations
   a. differentiation of specific properties
   b. grouping together objects somewhat related
   c. labeling or categorizing of items
II. Interpretation of data and making inferences
   a. assembling of information
   b. explaining reason for certain events
   c. drawing relevant inferences from data
   d. formulating a generalization or inference
III. Application of known principles and facts to explain new phenomena, to predict consequences from known conditions and events, or to develop hypotheses by using known generalizations and facts

a. predicting
b. establishing a pattern of relationships or information to test the validity of predictions

These processes are arranged roughly in order of complexity, and all involve various levels of abstraction and difficulty. Dr. Taba worked with teachers to help them develop a strategy for moving the pupils through these thought processes. Certain ideas evolved from her study which seem important if teachers are to be effective in developing thought processes. Some of her thoughts are

The "seeking" functions of teaching assume a greater importance than those of "giving." This reverses the usual role of the teacher.

The role of questions becomes crucial. The type of questions asked by the teacher limits or releases the mental operations performed, the points to be explored, and the modes of thought students learn.

Some pupils require a great deal more concrete information before being able to move to the next level of thinking.

Thus the teacher must time his questions used in the lifting of thought levels according to his diagnosis of the "readiness" of his class to move up to the next level of thinking. Attempts to lift thoughts prematurely may result in either confusion or regression.

The teacher must understand the structure and sequence of the thinking process and have a thorough understanding of the content being taught.

Four patterns of classroom discussion illustrate the problem the teacher has with "pacing" and lifting the discussion to a higher level. The numbers on the vertical scale represent thought levels. The horizontal scale represents continuing discussion.

Pattern A illustrates a type of discussion in which the teacher attempts to raise the level of thought very early in the discussion. Obviously discussion reverts continuously to a lower level. Pattern B illustrates Taba's recommended pattern

FIGURE 6–3
CLASS DISCUSSION PATTERNS

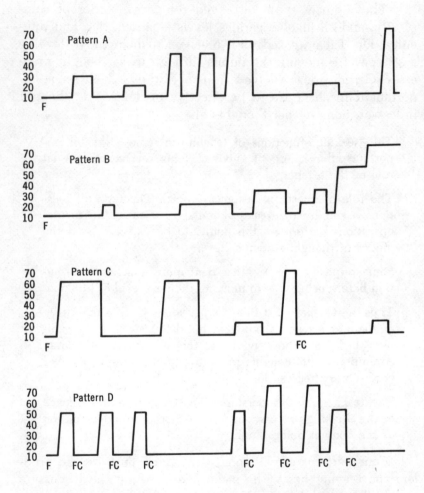

Hilda Taba and others. *Thinking in Elementary School Children.* Cooperative Research Project No. 1574. (San Francisco State College, San Francisco, 1964), p. 129.

for effective pacing. The level of seeking information is sustained for a considerable period of time. Grouping is requested only after a large amount of information has been accumulated.

The children then make fairly rapid progress from grouping to labeling, to providing reasons for labeling to inferences. Pattern C shows the teacher repeatedly attempting to steer discussion to a higher level without permitting the accumulation of information. The children repeatedly return to the information level. Pattern D represents a constant change of focus finally stabilizing on the primitive level.[4]

Significance of Such Studies

What is the significance of such intricate projects for you as a beginning teacher? These two studies are illustrations of current attempts to improve learning. Each of them emphasizes the role of the teacher as one who seeks to guide the thinking of children instead of continuously passing out information.

The way the reader sees his role as a teacher will determine the activities provided in the classroom. The activities will determine the way children learn. If he sees himself as an infallible dispenser of information, the chances are slight that there will be a change of behavior in ways of thinking or in developing values. Taba makes the point that teachers "who seek formal thinking more frequently also get it more frequently."[5]

The kind of questions the teacher asks either limits and restricts the response of the child or opens and lifts the response possibilities. As the reader visits classes he should listen carefully to the type of questions the teachers use and the responses of the children. He should analyze the results to see if he can determine the most productive type of questions. Similar analyses can be made of questions the instructors use in the college classes he attends.

As the reader progresses in his teacher training programs undoubtedly there will be a number of additional research studies which will further illuminate his role as a teacher.

[4]This section has been freely adapted from Hilda Taba, Samuel Levine, and Freeman F. Elzey, *Thinking in Elementary School Children*, Cooperative Research Project No. 1574, U.S. Office of Education (San Francisco State College, San Francisco, 1964), 207 pp.

[5]*Ibid.*, p. 177.

SUMMARY

The teaching-learning process is a complex one. The approaches used by the teacher, the questions asked, the skill utilized in eliciting pupils' responses, and the use of effective pacing all affect pupil learning. The emotional component of a teacher's response can either spur a child on to greater heights or make him withdraw more into his shell or drive him to strike out aggressively at the youngster across the aisle.

The major purpose of this chapter has been to give you some insight into the research being done. Examples of studies of classroom climate and classroom observations show that what the teacher does in the classroom can be improved. Suchman's Inquiry Training and Taba's study of thinking show that approaches and procedures used in the classroom can improve the learning of children.

SUGGESTED READINGS

Bany, Mary A. and Lois V. Johnson, *Classroom Group Behavior: Group Dynamics in Education*, The Macmillan Company, New York, 1964.

Points out basic understandings of the many dynamic forces that affect the class as a group. Offers suggested techniques for changing group behavior.

Bradfield, Luther E., *Supervision for Modern Elementary Schools*, Charles E. Merrill Books, Inc., Columbus, 1964.

Chapters V and VI discuss the improvement of learning conditions and learning experiences.

Bruner, Jerome S., *Toward a Theory of Instruction*, Harvard University Press, Cambridge, 1966.

A collection of essays concerned with the relationship between the growth of the intellect and the art of teaching.

Hyman, Ronald T., *Teaching*, Lippincott, Philadelphia, 1968.

Readings dealing with problems of classroom interaction-communication, cognitive development, emotional and social climate, games and aesthetics.

Inhelder, Bärbel and Jean Piaget, *The Growth of Logical Thinking From Childhood to Adolescence*, Basic Books, Inc., Publishers, 1958.

Attempts to isolate and describe the mental structures on which reasoning processes are based. Is concerned with the development and operation of logical thought.

Jackson, Philip W., *Life in the Classroom*, Holt, Rinehart, and Winston, New York, 1968.

A look at the reality of the elementary classroom. Chapters 1, 3 and 5 provide a fascinating way of looking at classrooms.

Laurendeau, Monique and Adrien Pinard, *Causal Thinking in the Child*, International Universities Press, Inc., New York, 1962.

Based upon systematic observation of a group of children over a period of time. Deals with the child's conception of reality and causality.

Raths, Louis E., Merrill Harmin, and Sidney B. Simon, *Values and Teaching*, Charles E. Merrill Books, Inc., Columbus, 1966.

Discusses the development of a theory of values, ways of putting such a theory into use, and classroom methods for clarifying values.

Suchman, J. Richard, *The Elementary School Training Program in Scientific Inquiry*, University of Illinois, 1962.

Discusses, on the basis of experimentation, the structure and function of inquiry, training in inquiry, and its application in problematic situations.

Wilhelms, Fred T., editor, *Evaluation As Feedback and Guide*, 1967 yearbook, Association for Supervision and Curriculum Development, Washington, D.C., 1967.

Suggests new approaches to the evaluation of the teaching-learning process.

CHAPTER

7

The
Changing Elementary School
Curriculum and Organization

The elementary school of today is in the process of change involving both curriculum and organization. These changes affect all phases of the elementary school; all learning materials for children, equipment, the role of teachers and administrators, the training of teachers, and the design of school buildings.

Three directions can be clearly identified. Content of what is to be taught is emphasizing important generalizations. The processes of learning are stressing discovery rather than rote learning. Individualization of instruction is becoming a reality through specially prepared materials, use of technology and new arrangements for utilizing staff.

The elementary school of tomorrow will undoubtedly be markedly different from today. As a prospective elementary teacher, the reader will be living with change throughout his professional career. Openness to new ideas and procedures, supported by a foundation for their evaluation is a must for the elementary teacher of the future.

NEW CURRICULUM DEVELOPMENTS

Today elementary schools are faced with more proposals for changing the curriculum than have been suggested in the last thirty years. The period from 1930 to 1957 could be characterized by the introduction of unit teaching, emphasis on concepts and generalizations, use of community resources, improved textbooks, increased availability and use of audiovisual aids, increased application of the accumulating knowledge of child development, research studies on methods of teaching, and social utility studies especially in arithmetic and spelling. Progress in improved educational programs had been slow but definite.

In the 50's a wave of education concern swept the nation. This concern was greatly accelerated by the launching of Sputnik by the Russians in 1957. Money in quantities unimagined a few years previously was made available to strengthen our educational programs. The National Defense Educational Act and the National Science Foundation supplied government funds; foundations such as the Ford Fund for Advancement in Education sponsored many demonstration projects.

One result was the utilization of the competencies of scholars in the various disciplines to help update the curriculum of both the elementary and secondary schools. The first of such attempts was known as PSSC, the Physical Science Study Committee, initiated in 1956. The purpose was to show pupils the structure of modern physics and how the structure was discovered. PSSC produced a complete "package" including a text, laboratory experiments, simplified apparatus, films, tests, supplementary references, and teachers' guides. The Committee also established a number of summer institutes to train teachers to use the material, and a program was telecast over a national network for upgrading teachers' and others' knowledge of modern physics. Outstanding scholars in physics worked with teachers and educators to produce the materials.

Many recent projects have followed a comparable pattern. The focus has been primarily on content, though some developments such as those described in Chapter 6 by Suchman and Taba emphasize process.

Most of the newer proposals seem to have the following elements in common:

1. The organization evolves from identifying the elements of

the discipline essential to understanding the structure of the discipline. (In contrast to use of contemporary life situations or questions and concerns of students).

2. The procedure emphasizes concepts, generalizations and processes.

3. The processes principally used provide opportunity for inquiry and discovery by the learner (in contrast to memorization.)

4. Content has been radically restructured in most subjects. Many concepts and generalizations have been presented sooner in the life of the child than was previously thought possible.

Descriptions of the newer programs can be found in the references in the bibliography at the end of this chapter: Alexander, A.S.C.D. *New Curriculum Developments*, and Michaelis and others.

If your library has a collection of curriculum materials, you should examine the newer curriculum materials and the teacher strategies suggested for presenting them in the classroom.

The curriculum requires two types of planning. The basic strategy is planned well in advance, utilizing individuals who have extensive background in a particular area of culture and who understand how children learn and develop. Such planning requires that scholars, teachers, and educators work cooperatively. The second type of planning is done in the local school by the teacher or teaching team. This requires the specific selection in each situation based on immediate needs and concerns of children. Obviously the choices made for a second-grade class of superior intelligence and high socio-economic backgrounds would be different from those made for a second-grade group of children with limited backgrounds and a culturally different environment.

One major problem has yet to be solved by the newer programs and that problem is one of balance for the individual child. The programs have developed from a single discipline approach, such as in mathematics and science, or a multi-discipline one as in social studies. None have evolved a total program for the elementary school.

As a teacher, assuming the reader has the best programs in each subject area, he would still have the responsibility for deciding what adaptations and additions are needed. The stress on the intellectual development does not minimize responsibilities in providing for the emotional and social development of the child. Improved intellectual functioning must be accompanied by improved emotional and social functioning.

THE CHANGING ORGANIZATION

Changes are taking place in the organization of the elementary school as well as in every other phase of elementary education. The purpose of any organizational scheme is to facilitate instruction, but organization should not become so complex and cumbersome a vehicle that its operation diverts energy and attention from that purpose.

"Why concern myself with problems of organization, since it will be several years before I will be teaching?" you ask. The answer is that some of the newer forms of organization require different competencies for teachers than are needed in the usual self-contained classroom. Having some understanding of some of the newer organizational plans will enable you to observe classes in schools with such plans and to discuss with the teachers the types of problems with which they deal.

Ideally the child should enter kindergarten and progress through grade six, *continuously* learning as he goes. It is only too easy to think fallaciously about the elementary school program as a race track, the same distance (content) to be covered by all the runners. In any race some horses, cars, or men cover the track faster than others.

A change in organization in and of itself will not be a cure-all. There must be improvement in the ways teachers see it is possible to work with children. In evaluating any new organizational pattern certain questions are crucial. Does the plan:

1. Provide for continuous learning for children?
2. Provide opportunities for richer and more significant learning experiences for children?

3. Free teachers to better know, relate with, and guide their children?

4. Provide for a better use of the talents of the staff of a school in improving the learning of children?

There are a number of different organizational plans being discussed. It is not surprising that the novice has difficulty understanding them for their proliferation can confuse the experienced individual as well. One source of confusion arises from the failure to differentiate between vertical and horizontal aspects of school organization.

> Schools are organized to serve specific functions. They must classify students and move them upward from a point of admission to a point of departure. Vertical organization serves this function. Schools also must divide the student body among available teachers. Horizontal organization serves this second function.[1]

Confusion is not entirely dispelled by this differentiation, for many of the newer plans involve elements of both horizontal and vertical reorganizations.

A second source of confusion is one of terminology and labels. It is easy for school systems to tack a popular label on their reorganizational plan. Two schools labeled non-graded may, and often do, differ widely in their method of grouping pupils.

School people also find it difficult to agree on terminology. The term "team teaching" is also known as "team organization, cooperative teaching, or team organization and planning." Undoubtedly other labels will be proposed to add to the semantic tangle.

Currently the two proposals receiving the most attention are the non-graded proposals, a vertical plan, and team teaching, a plan primarily involving horizontal reorganization. Each of these will be discussed in some detail. Harold Shane has described thirty-two plans of grouping which have been used

[1]John I. Goodlad, and Kenneth Rehage, "Unscrambling the Vocabulary of School Organization," *National Education Association Journal*, Vol. 51 (November, 1962), p. 34.

in the past century or are in current use.[2] The plans of the past were developed to cope with individual differences in pupils and to utilize teacher talents more effectively. Today's "new" plans often embody elements of past organizational proposals, tried and now forgotten. A reading of Shane's article will help develop some historical perspective in current proposals.

In studying any plan of organization it is important to reiterate that organization exists to facilitate instruction. The final evaluation of any plan is whether or not it facilitates learning on the part of the children. As our current research results on various organizational plans are studied, the present conclusion seems to indicate that the type of organization makes relatively little difference in the learning of the children. Too often, however, comparative studies have been inadequate in answering the questions which should be asked. We are not only concerned about the effect of the organizational plan on the average student but also on the bright student, on the slow child, on the isolate, on the anxious child, and on the culturally deprived. Most of the current research does not give us answers in these areas.

VERTICAL ORGANIZATION

Graded School

The organizational plan in vogue since 1848 is known as the graded school. The usual elementary school includes Kindergarten and grades one through six or grades one through eight. Most frequently a teacher has only one grade in a class. In a large school there may be several first-grade teachers and several second-grade teachers. The children are assigned to grades upon entrance to school at age six or thereabouts and continue to progress one grade a year unless they are failed. Teachers attempt to cover during the year what they consider to be the curriculum of that grade.

At the time the graded plan was put into effect in the

[2]Harold G. Shane, "Grouping in the Elementary School," *Phi Delta Kappan*, Vol. 41 (April, 1960), pp. 313–319.

Quincy Grammar School in Boston in 1848 we knew little about individual differences in children. Intelligence tests were not used until after World War I. In the graded school the child was failed if he did not successfully complete the material for the grade.

Throughout the years, criticisms of the graded school have mounted. A variety of plans has been tried such as the Dalton and Winnetka individual study plans. However, the graded school has continued until the present time. The major adjustment has been to decrease the failure rate by attempts to provide for the wide range of individual differences in each class. Most teachers today are apt to have three reading groups in the room: slow, average, and fast. Ability grouping is another method of attempting to meet the problem of individual differences where several rooms of the same grade exist. There will be a class of slow children, a class of average children, and one of bright children. One of the major difficulties of such a grouping is that if reading ability is used for grouping, there still will be about as wide a range of achievement in each class in all of the other subjects, such as arithmetic. If intelligence is used for grouping, the range in reading or arithmetic is decreased only slightly. Grouping was popular a number of years ago. At one time on the basis of research findings it was abandoned, but recently some school administrators see it as a panacea, and it has been revived. Actually it is opposed by most experts in elementary education.

Nongraded School

The first nongraded or ungraded school with multi-age groups was the one room school. One agile teacher taught all grades, all subjects, and had the additional responsibility for seeing that the pot-bellied stove was kept stoked. The first nongraded school, as we currently define the term, is credited as having its beginnings in Western Springs, Illinois, in 1934. It was later abandoned. Milwaukee in 1942 began and has continued the primary nongraded school. The movement has been greatly accelerated since about the middle 1950's.

A nongraded school is simply a school which has eliminated formal grade barriers. Although some experimentation has been carried out in the secondary schools, the most extensive experimentation has been in the primary grades. A child is not said to be in the first grade but rather in Miss Smith's room. In some schools a child may continue in Miss Smith's room for two or three years, progressing at his own rate. In other schools the primary block is organized around levels of reading ability. Miss Smith might have levels one, two, and three in her room. When Jimmy had completed level three, he would be put in Miss Jones' room, who has levels three, four, and five.

The essence of all the nongraded plans is to enable the child to progress at his own rate, not to be impeded by slower pupils or jostled ahead by the pacesetters. While most children complete the primary block in three years, some children might make it in two, others might require four. Some students of elementary education question the substitution of nine to eleven reading levels for three grades. The arguments in education literature for and against nongraded schools have been summarized by Stuart Dean; as can be seen, some of these arguments are subjective and not necessarily valid or conclusive. Can you spot some of the emotionally toned statements?

ARGUMENTS FOR THE NONGRADED SCHOOL

1. Recognition of and provision for individual differences among children
2. Flexibility in administrative structure
3. Abolition of artificial barriers of grades and promotion
4. Respect for the continuity and interrelatedness of learning
5. Student progress commensurate with ability
6. Improved mental health for both teachers and students
7. Stimulation for major curricular revision
8. Harmony with the educational objectives of a democratic society
9. Administrative feasibility for all levels and age groups.
10. Schools program-oriented rather than operationally controlled

ARGUMENTS AGAINST NONGRADED SCHOOLS

1. Soft pedagogy, lacking fixed standards and requirements

2. Impossible burden on teachers
3. Replacement of grade requirements by reading levels
4. Lack of pupil progress and information to parents
5. Inadequacy and insufficiency of teacher preparation
6. Absence of minimal standards and expectancies for all children
7. Lack of specificity and order in curriculum sequence
8. "An improved means to an unimproved end"—Thoreau
9. Uncertainty that improved teaching will result
10. Widespread misuse and abuse of terminology of non-gradedness[3]

Actually there is wide variety in various nongraded plans, but research has been inconclusive as to the values. The best reference for further reading is John Goodlad and Robert Anderson, *The Nongraded Elementary School.*[4] The basic concept of providing for continuous progress in the children's learning is an admittedly commendable objective. However, there is some danger that the content of the primary block may be as rigidly conceived as in the graded school. In such a case the rate of progressing through the block would be the only advantage.

"How should my training be different if I were to be assigned to a class in a nongraded school?" Actually your attitudes, not your training, would be different. You would feel that you were free to help each child to progress at his own rate. You could adapt materials to the level of the child. These same feelings should permeate the graded school, but too often the concept of grade levels seem to inhibit rather than release.

HORIZONTAL ORGANIZATION

Vertical organization provides the two major alternatives, graded and nongraded. Horizontal organization permits many alternatives involving arranging of children, curriculum, or teacher competencies. John I. Goodlad and Kenneth Rehage have outlined the possibilities.

If the primary consideration in establishing a pattern of

[3]Stuart E. Dean, "Nongraded Schools," *Education Briefs*, U.S. Office of Education, Washington, D.C., July, 1964.
[4]Revised edition (Harcourt, Brace & World, Inc., New York, 1963).

horizontal organization is children, then a choice must be made between homogeneity (likeness) and heterogeneity (difference) in pupils comprising each class group. If the choice is for homogeneity, the criterion of likeness may be age, size, interest, ability, achievement, or a combination of these and other factors. If the primary consideration is the curriculum, a choice may be made between separate subjects and various combinations of subjects as the basis for setting up class groups. If the primary consideration is teacher qualification, one choice is between the self-contained classroom (one teacher for all subjects) and departmentalization (a different teacher for each subject).[5]

Team Organization

A challenging innovation in the current wave of educational reform is known as team teaching. It is primarily horizontal organization of the school. It involves grouping of children, considerations of curriculum, and teacher talents.

Team teaching is a type of instructional organization, involving teaching personnel and the student assigned to them, in which two or more teachers, working together, are given responsibility for all or a significant part of the instruction of the same group of students.[6]

Basically several teachers work together for the instruction of the same group of students. This represents a radical departure from one teacher having sole control of learning in one classroom, too often with little communication with other teachers.

This pattern of school organization started with a few pilot projects around 1956. It has spread very rapidly, assisted by support and publicity given by the Ford Fund for Advancement of Education. The Committee on Staff Utilization of the National Association of Secondary School Principals has been sponsoring many projects. The idea has also spread to a large number of elementary schools. Some newer elementary school

[5]John I. Goodlad and Kenneth Rehage, *op. cit.*, p. 35.
[6]Judson T. Shaplin and Henry F. Olds, Jr., eds., *Team Teaching* (Harper and Row, Publishers, New York, 1964), p. 15.

buildings have been designed to facilitate team teaching. If you are near such a school, be sure to visit it.

The make-up of teams of teachers varies greatly in number of teachers, number of students, and number of grades involved. Other differences include methods of grouping pupils, the extent to which small and large groups are used, and the extent to which real changes have occurred in the curriculum and instructional procedures.

No organizational plan will guarantee improved learning on the part of children. Extremely careful evaluation should be made of the educational growth of children of varying abilities, backgrounds, and personality patterns. Such studies are difficult and complex. To a veteran observer of trends and innovations it would appear that more money and effort have gone into publicizing programs than to evaluating them, although there are encouraging beginnings of evaluation.

The plans vary from two teachers working together informally with 50 or 60 pupils to highly organized teams with specified levels of responsibility. Such a team would include a team leader, senior teachers, other teachers, student teachers, and aides of various sorts. Often in the more structured situation the team leader receives extra pay.

Among the advantages claimed for team teaching are better instruction, better teaching procedures, more profitable use of building space, better use of the special talents and time of individual teachers, better use of instructional aids, and improved supervision (by a team leader). It cannot be too strongly stressed that no organizational plan by itself will assure such results. It may facilitate achievement of some of these improvements, but a tremendous amount of teacher and administrative effort must be devoted to each area.

Team teaching requires more work on the part of teachers. Many of the decisions formerly administrative, such as grouping and scheduling, must be done by the team. While flexibility is possible in arranging pupils in large and small groups for purposes of instruction, it is easy to develop complicated schedules which may become rigid.

One of the arguments raised against team teaching is that

teachers cannot get to know their pupils as well as in a self-contained classroom. When a team works with a new group of pupils each year, it certainly is not as easy to know 90 pupils as 30. However, where a team is organized vertically over several grades and has the same pupils for several years, the problem is lessened. There are some advantages in several teachers working with a problem pupil, because each one sees the pupil somewhat differently. On the other hand, limited conference time might be over-directed to the slow, the gifted, and the disturbingly aggressive who would thus receive the major benefit from the pooling of teachers' judgments.

Evaluation of the actual accomplishments of team teaching have been limited due to recency of the program, lack of funds for evaluation, inadequate measuring instruments, and rather meager research designs. Glen Heathers has summarized the present research.

From his data it would seem that:

It is possible to select, train, and utilize aides (subprofessional personnel) effectively.

Some teachers seem unsuited for team teaching. (We don't know why.)

Teachers work harder. (This may be due to the problems of change.)

It seemingly is a catalytic agent for bringing about changes in curricula, audio-visual materials, instructional techniques and teacher cooperation.

There seems to be little difference in achievement as measured by conventional tests between team teaching and more traditional plans of organization. Research has not made comparisons for pupils of different ability levels or personality patterns.

Studies dealing with the personal-social adjustment of pupils show no evidence that harm has occurred under team teaching.[7]

There is very limited evidence which shows that for some

[7]*Ibid.*, Chapter 10.

indicators of personal adjustment of pupils, team teaching is somewhat superior.

Training Needed to Do Team Teaching

"How should my training differ for starting as a team teacher rather than in a self contained classroom?" you might ask. This list is not in order of importance.

1. Obtain sufficient training in one subject area so you have a strong background in that area. This will probably mean concentrating your electives in one area.
2. Become familiar with learning materials and equipment for conducting both individual programs of study and also those for large classes.
3. Become familiar with special methods for teaching students to achieve such goals as critical thinking, inquiry, creativity, self-instruction and self-evaluation. (All teachers need this, but it is a special need for team teachers.)
4. Understand processes of group work. Often sociology or psychology offer courses in this area which are of value.
5. Seek opportunities to work with pupils in small and large groups. Start with small groups.
6. Utilize opportunities to work with colleagues in planning instructional units.
7. Utilize opportunities to participate with colleagues in considering personal-social adjustment problems of pupils.
8. Accept a student teaching assignment involving team teaching where possible.[8]

OTHER METHODS OF IMPROVED STAFF UTILIZATION

Relief from the heavy load of clerical and routine duties of the teacher has been provided in some cases by teacher aids, secretaries and/or a technician to produce visual aids.

The extent to which special subject teaching and consultants is available depends upon the school system. Some schools have consultants in art, music, physical education, library and foreign language. In certain cases these consultants work with

[8]Some of the ideas were suggested by Glen Heathers, *Ibid.*, Chapter 10.

teachers, in others they do direct teaching. In addition, in the central administrative office, there are supervisors in the special subject areas.

Some school systems have many specialized personnel, including school nurses, doctors, psychologists, speech correctionists, social workers, counselors for elementary schools, and audio-visual experts. Small school systems may have only a general elementary supervisor, and some may have no consultant help. When joining the staff of a new system, one should become informed as soon as possible about the consultative help available if the orientation program for the newcomer does not provide this background in detail.

THE LARGER ORGANIZATION

When the reader signs his first contract to teach, he will be a member of a larger organization. Every organization has a formal structure which a chart can picture. The lines of authority are clearly designated. The teacher in an elementary school is responsible to the principal, the principal to an assistant superintendent or superintendent, the superintendent to the local Board of Education, the Board to the people of the community who usually are responsible for electing them.

All fifty states have state departments of public instruction under various names. There are a number of state regulations governing the operation of the local school districts. Some of these may be laws of the state legislature, others rules of the state departments. The local school boards have considerable freedom to determine salaries, appoint personnel, approve curricula, purchase instructional material, and formulate policies for local operations. The educational system of the United States is decidedly decentralized when compared to the national systems of other countries.

The reader's class may be interested in investigating the plan of organization of his state department. The method of financing education is another topic worth a class report.

The larger a school system, the more procedures are formalized. Conversely, the smaller the system the more personal-ized are the procedures. Frustrations in the larger districts are likely to be with the "system" and in the smaller with individuals.

Non-certified personnel such as the custodian, school secretary, and cafeteria workers are an important part of the staff. They are respected members of the team in helping the school provide a better program for children. Only a very gauche beginner would consider them otherwise.

SUMMARY

The curriculum of tomorrow is going to be markedly different from that of today. In our concern for curriculum and organizational changes we must never lose sight of the elementary classroom as a place where children of different abilities, backgrounds, and rates of development live and grow in an encouraging atmosphere. Pressures on teachers and schools should not be passed on to pupils. Our desire to produce better mathematics should not crowd out creative experiences. Our need for orderly procedures should not result in an atmosphere where the child feels safe only when he is conforming. The elementary school needs to be a challenging, growing, and exciting place for each child. What we know about the way children grow and develop should be incorporated, not sacrificed, in curriculum innovations. We as teachers need to be open to new experience and willing to experiment. Our careers should never become more reminiscent than they are dynamic.

It is impossible to predict the organizational pattern of the elementary school in which the reader will do his first teaching. Wide experimentation is under way with new plans of organization or variations of old plans. Such changes involve considerable preparation and planning by the staff. This is no day and age for either young or old fogies who cling for security to ossified lesson plans.

Too often it seems that systems are busily adopting a new organizational plan as a means of being on the "bandwagon." Such plans should be carefully evaluated in terms of providing

(1) continuous learning for pupils, (2) more significant learning experiences (improved curriculum and teaching methods), (3) ways teachers can know, relate with, and guide their pupils, and (4) a more effective use of the talents of the staff.

Changes can be vertical or horizontal or combinations of both. The vertical plan which seems most promising is that of the nongraded elementary school. The most promising horizontal plan, known as team teaching, involves new ways of grouping pupils and utilizing teachers' talents more effectively.

Team teaching has definite implications for the need of developing new patterns for the training of elementary school teachers. If the plan is widely adopted, new elementary school buildings will be much different from the usual ones which include only standardized size rooms, a library, an office, and a multipurpose room.

SUGGESTED READINGS

Alexander, William M., *Changing Curriculum Content.* Report of the Conference on Curriculum Content, 1963, Association for Supervision and Curriculum Development, Washington, D.C., 1964.

Discusses the changing emphases in curriculum and instruction, including the impact of new projects on the school program.

Anderson, Robert H., *Teaching in a World of Change*, Harcourt, Brace and World, New York, 1966.

Describes innovations in organization.

Association for Supervision and Curriculum Development, *New Curriculum Developments.* The Association, Washington, D.C., 1965.

An excellent discussion of new curriculum developments in education by an outstanding group of people from different fields. Chapter I on the case for change and Chapter XI on problems and prospects of current curriculum development are very informative.

Association for Supervision and Curriculum Development, *Using Current Curriculum Developments.* The Association, Washington, D.C., 1963.

Experts from various subject fields interpret research and curriculum innovations in their respective fields. Chapter XI is concerned with learning theory.

Crosby, Muriel, *Curriculum Development for Elementary Schools in a Changing Society.* D. C. Heath & Company, Boston, 1964.
Chapter VI discusses the foundations of curriculum development. Chapter VII is concerned with assessing the effectiveness of the curriculum. Emphasis throughout is upon change taking place and what it means to the school.

Department of Elementary School Principals, *The National Elementary Principal,* Vol. 44, No. 3. January, 1965, Washington, D.C., Department of Elementary School Principals, National Education Association.
This entire issue is devoted to team teaching. An excellent condensation of the concept.

Goodlad, John I. (ed.), *The Changing American School.* The 65th Yearbook of the National Society for the Study of Education, Part II, The University of Chicago Press, Chicago, 1966.
Chapter II discusses the curriculum. Chapter V discusses the forces and ideas that are reshaping school organization and the extent and significance of reorganization. Chapter VI analyzes the physical factors of the school building in relation to the curriculum.

Goodlad, John I. and Robert H. Anderson, *The Nongraded Elementary School,* rev. ed., Harcourt, Brace & World, Inc., New York, 1963.
The emergence of the nongraded school, its operation, its establishment, and its future are covered.

Goodlad, John I., *School Curriculum Reform in the United States,* Fund for the Advancement of Education, New York, 1964.
Brief looks at some of the modern curriculum programs developed in recent years. Conclusions and recommendations are offered.

Lee, J. Murray and Dorris May Lee, *The Child and His Curriculum,* Appleton-Century-Crofts, New York, 1960.
This book deals with all areas of interest in elementary teaching. New trends in the various areas are indicated and the bibliographies are extensive and helpful.

Manolakes, George, *The Elementary School We Need,* Commission on Elementary Curriculum, Association for Supervision and Curriculum Development, Washington, D.C., 1965.

This forty-page pamphlet should be read by every prospective teacher. Chapters III and IV set forth guides for instruction and describe how these are translated into practice.

McLoughlin, William P., "The Phantom Nongraded School," *Phi Delta Kappan*, XLIX, No. 5 (January, 1968), 248–250.

Mr. McLoughlin concludes that true non-gradedness has seldom been tried although up to 30 percent of the U.S. districts report doing so.

Michaelis, John U., Ruth Grossman, and Lloyd F. Scott, *New Designs for the Elementary School Curriculum*, McGraw-Hill Book Company, New York, 1967.

The most comprehensive description and discussion of newer curriculum programs.

Miller, Richard, *The Nongraded School, Analysis and Study*, Harper and Row Publishers, New York, 1967.

Sixteen experts have provided an excellent analysis of the non-graded school.

National Education Association, *Schools for the 60's*, McGraw-Hill Book Company, New York, 1963.

Chapter 3 discusses the organization of all aspects of the school for more effective teaching and learning.

Shaplin, Judson T. and Henry F. Olds, Jr. (eds.), *Team Teaching*, Harper and Row, Publishers, New York, 1964.

Defines, describes and presents a rationale for team teaching. Discusses also the role of the teacher and how the curriculum would function. An extensive bibliography is provided.

Snyder, Edith Roach, *The Self-Contained Classroom*, Association for Supervision and Curriculum Development, Washington, D.C., 1960.

An excellent collection of short articles on implementing the self-contained classroom.

Spitzer, Herbert F., *Teaching Elementary School Mathematics*, Houghton Mifflin Company, Boston, 1968, 373 pp.

This book describes and analyzes current methods of teaching the "new math" in elementary schools. The approach emphasizes student thinking and inquiry.

Thalen, Herbert A., *Education and the Human Quest*, Harper and Row, Publishers, New York, 1960.

Laments the failure to utilize what is known about the nature of man, knowledge, the dynamics of learning, factors affecting group performance, and others. Stresses importance and value of inquiry as a way to learn.

Thomas, George I. and Joseph Crescimbeni, *Individualizing Instruction in the Elementary School*, Random House, New York, 1967.

Excellent suggestions for individualizing instructions in each of the subject fields.

8

Technology
Improves Learning

One need not leave home to see overwhelming evidence of modern technology. If economic well-being permits, a home may have an automatic dishwasher, laundry unit of washer and dryer, vacuum cleaner, floor scrubber with waxing and polishing attachments, a stove with baffling electronic controls, completely automatic refrigerator and freezer, and a central heating and cooling unit calculated to outwit the weather. One may also scrape the whiskers, dry the hair, perk the coffee, toast the toast, and brush the teeth with electrical gadgets.

Occasionally a courageous but ill-advised male suggests that the technological advances in the home have eliminated the work of the housewife. His foolhardiness is compounded if he adds that in the good old days his grandmother raised nine children and had no resources but the wood stove and the dish pan, the washtub, and a corrugated iron object called a washboard. He may count himself fortunate if he escapes with a mild reminder that the electrical cooking, cleaning, and laundry devices have yet to be seen running themselves by remote control. An articulate wife can outline in detail the manner in which her work is expedited, and it is safe to assume that there will be no nostalgic return to the washboard when the discussion is ended.

Every new technological device for the classroom has aroused concern that the teacher would be eliminated and that education would go forward by means of depersonalized button pushing. These consistently gloomy predictions have just as consistently been ignored by self-starting teachers who find extended resources and reduction of lost motion in effective use of teaching aids.

The housewife with a modern washing machine has a marvelously sensitive instrument that will handle everything from a delicate blouse to a load of work clothes. Or more accurately, it will do its intended job if the housewife reads the owner's manual and carefully follows the directions for handling temperature, water flow, and spinning speed.

Teachers with film projectors, tape recorders, overhead projectors, and other devices can add an exciting dimension to their work, but not until they learn to operate these resources for maximum efficiency. Some teacher-education programs require a course in audio-visual aids while other institutions provide individual opportunities for learning to operate the equipment. A beginning teacher who avoids this area of preparation is a wood stove and washboard thinker.

TELEVISION

In and out of school viewing has dramatically expanded the classroom to encompass the world. Satellites such as Telstar routinely supply live telecasts from most parts of the world, and into the classroom and living rooms come the great events of the world. Yesterday's teachers had few means of extending the boundaries of their classrooms. The teachers of today and tomorrow will have no excuse for xenophobia.

Children spend a surprising amount of time (three hours) watching television each day. Northwestern University's Paul A. Witty who has been following viewing habits of children since 1950 reports:

> TV has been with us about a decade and one-half. During that time, it has become children's favored leisure pursuit and has had a marked influence on their behavior and at-

titudes. TV consumes about 21 hours each week of children's time. But it is not alone among the mass media in this respect. Radio also takes an average of 7 to 8 hours each week. Children go to the movies outside the home, on the average, about once every two or three weeks. Their reading, on the whole, is meager and consumes about one-third as much time as TV.[1]

There are many possibilities for utilizing home viewing in the classroom.

Direct Classroom Telecasts

Two methods are used, the open circuit and the closed circuit. By far the most popular is the open circuit program which can be received by any classroom in the viewing area. Direct telecasts have been attempted in practically every subject taught in the elementary school. So far the testing which has been done has indicated that television classes do at least as well as regular classes on the items measured by the tests.

The value of television lessons obviously depends upon the quality of the lesson. An outstanding teacher must be used, visuals be prepared by expert technicians, and the program be carefully planned to supplement the curriculum of the classroom. Most programs supplement and enrich classroom experiences; some, however, such as the teaching of a foreign language, carry the major burden of direct teaching. The direct teaching programs such as foreign languages, and in some cases art and music, provide their own "pacing" of learning and can be adapted to the classroom without difficulty. Other areas such as social studies have more complicated problems of correlating with the curriculum. A large city producing its own programs can easily develop social studies programs which correlate directly with the curriculum at a specific grade level. However, an educational television station reaching a large number of school systems with variation in their third grade social studies curriculum has a different problem.

For most telecasts, a teacher's manual is available. The

[1]Paul A. Witty, Paul Kinsella, and Anne Coomer, "A Summary of Yearly Studies of Televiewing 1949–1963," *Elementary English*, Volume 40 (October, 1963), p. 596.

most complete manuals include suggestions for class projects, outlines of the telecast, questions to be asked, and suggestions for supplementary art, music, and reading activities.

It is not mandatory that television programs, films, film strips, and tapes be utilized by the whole class. Individuals or small groups can often make effective use of such aids. An example of this type of programming was the Midwest Program on Airborne Television Instruction (MPATI) for the gifted pupils in grades 5 and 6 in arithmetic.

Another function television can serve is to improve the quality of teaching. An outstanding example is Alice Swartz' program entitled "Art and You," telecast over Southern Illinois University's educational television station, WSIU, for primary children. This program in 1964 won first place in the fine arts and humanities area in the Institute for Education by Radio and Television at Ohio State University. It is the opinion of administrators in the schools using the program that the quality of art instruction has greatly improved.

Another possibility in the future is that sets will be so equipped that a teacher will be able to run his own tapes on the set in his classroom. This development is now possible but has not been made available commercially. If the reader's college or university has an educational television station, a tour of its facilities would be most interesting. He should try to observe a class using educational television.

PROJECTION POSSIBILITIES

Modern technology has provided the teacher with numerous possibilities for using projected materials. Included are the 8 or 16 mm sound or silent film, the film strip in sound or silent, the 3½" × 4" picture slide, the 2" × 2" slides, flat pictures using the opaque projector, transparencies using the overhead projector, microscope slides using the micro-projector, individual stereographic viewers and microfilms, and micro-cards using an individual microviewer. There is also the tachistoscope which regulates the time the exposure is on the screen with speeds up to 1/100 of a second.

Some newer developments include the magnetic sound film projector which is actually a combination of a 16 mm sound motion picture projector and tape recorder. We can expect commercial films to be produced in such a way that the teacher can record voice or sound. Such a machine also permits voice or sound to be added to a locally produced silent film. Polaroid has made it possible to make a 3½″ × 4″ slide in a few minutes. Thermofax has also produced relatively inexpensive equipment for quickly making transparencies for use on the overhead projector.

Each of these visual aids can be utilized in the classroom to serve somewhat different purposes. The 16 mm films and film strips have been used for some time, and there is a large supply of commercially available films which enrich classroom learning. It is advisable to preview as many films suited to your grade as possible. The popularity of the miniature camera and the 2″ × 2″ colored slides provide rich sources of material. Individuals with slide collections are often delighted to find a new, if young, audience which is not yet jaded by too frequent exposure to travel slides.

The overhead projectors are becoming increasingly popular as the price decreases and the imagination of the user increases. The teacher can write or draw directly on acetate rolls while facing the class or make his own transparencies easily. There is an increasing commercial supply of transparencies often involving several overlays. It is possible even to obtain an animated effect with the use of polarized light. Color transparencies can be "lifted" from many magazines. Opaque objects can be used and will project as dark shapes. Additional suggested uses are map projections, reading charts, and a child's story to illustrate handwriting or language usage.

You must be able to thread a 16 mm projector and operate the most commonly used pieces of equipment. It would be helpful if you learned how to make transparencies and slides. You need to be familiar with as much of the commercially produced material as possible. Above all you need to utilize your imagination as to the ways these resources can be utilized to improve and enrich learning. There are a number of excellent professional books in the audio-visual field which will assist you in all of these areas.

AUDIO POSSIBILITIES

Audio facilities include educational radio, records and transcriptions, the tape recorder, and language laboratories. Educational radio programs are still available in some parts of the country, although they are being rapidly replaced by educational television. Language laboratories are primarily used in the secondary schools in teaching a foreign language. Here the student can listen to the correct pronunciation, try to pronounce words himself, and compare his results with the original. Modifications of the usual language laboratory might include visually projected material and be used in teaching reading. If possible visit a language laboratory. There are undoubtedly several in operation by the foreign language department of your institution.

Recordings have become increasingly available since the development of the 33⅓ r.p.m. disk. Included are dramatizations of important historical events, actual voices of important contemporary persons, authors reading selections of their works, many children's stories, and of course a wide variety of musical records. Recently Laurence Senesh of Purdue University produced a number of transcriptions for use in teaching economic understandings to first grade children. Think of the motivation of listening to the voices of Roosevelt and Churchill, of Robert Frost and Vachel Lindsay. Also becoming increasingly available are the sound film strips with accompanying records.

Here again is the problem of getting acquainted with as much of this material as possible. Most colleges have record collections useful in the elementary school, and the reader can listen on his own time in the privacy of a listening booth. How do you think listening booths in connection with an elementary school library could be used?

The tape recorder is one of the most useful, if not the most useful, of the electronic devices for the creative and imaginative teacher.The reader's own imagination is practically the only limitation to developing uses of the tape recorder. Children can evaluate their own oral reports which have been taped. Speech mannerisms can be more easily corrected. Exchange of tapes with other schools would provide unusual material in the social studies. A child can listen to his own oral reading, and samples of oral reading tapes over the year would supply a basis for teacher-parent conferences. Music offers many possibilities. One student council even recorded the noise in the halls and played it back to a student assembly.

As the reader observes in classrooms, he should imagine and keep a list of the possibilities of using the tape recorder both for classroom and individual instruction.

PROGRAMMED LEARNING

Programmed learning is one of the most recent and rapidly developing techniques to appear on the educational scene. Essentially it is a process of supplying the learner with a step-by-step sequence of questions to which he responds. As the learner moves to the next question, he is able to determine whether his answer to the previous question was correct or not. He is able to work ahead at his own pace, always knowing how correct his answers are. It is as though each pupil were supplied a tutor who would say "You are correct," or "You are wrong, try again," in a neutral voice. Imagine a teacher who would never get impatient, cross, elated, or depressed—one who would never want to hurry a child. Programmed learning supplies such a teacher.

Programs are presented in programmed texts or in teaching machines. The teaching machines vary from very simple devices presenting only reading materials to highly complex machines using print, slides, film strips, motion picture film, and tape recordings. Programmed texts seem to be the most popular development for the elementary school. Since the programmed text is "bulkier" than the regular texts, more space is needed to develop a good program; hence the project is more expensive. Computers are now being used experimentally.

The beginning of the basic idea of teaching by machines is generally credited to S. L. Pressey prior to 1920. However, little interest was shown by others in his suggestions. The present explosion of interest is due to B. F. Skinner, an experimental psychologist at Harvard University. One of his first articles appeared in 1954.[2] At the present time the interest in programmed learning is tremendous as it involves industry, the military, experimental psychologists, publishers, and companies producing machines. Programs range from teaching illiterates, kindergarten, and first grade through the most complex graduate subjects.

There are two basic types of programming, the "linear," recommended by Skinner, and the "branching," proposed by N. A. Crowder. A linear program is composed of small steps, "frames" of questions, progressing logically step by step through the subject. It is important that the steps be so small that the learner can be successful at each step.

The branching program presents the learner with a problem and several answers. When he selects an answer he is referred to another frame. If correct, the frame presents another problem and he continues. If incorrect, the frame to which he is then referred tells him why he was wrong. Then the student is put through a series of frames to correct his error or returned to the original problem. Programs are now appearing using a mixture of both types. Writing out the responses required in the linear program has certain values in learning, and allowing brighter students to progress at a more rapid rate is a marked value of the branching program.

Advantages of programmed learning are:

Some students have been able to learn factual information at a more rapid rate.

Children can learn at their own pace.

The pupil's work is immediately evaluated by himself rather than by others. This may improve the self concept of the child. We do not know its result at the present time.

Teachers can be freed to give additional time to individual-

[2] B. F. Skinner, "The Science of Learning and the Art of Teaching," *Harvard Educational Review*, Vol. 24 (Spring, 1954), pp. 86–97.

ized instruction and enriching the experiences of the classroom. We have no studies as to whether teachers make more effective use of time.

Special programs will be developed for providing enrichment material for the gifted which will be self teaching and remedial materials for the slow learner.

It may be that programmed materials will have special value for the highly anxious child. We do not know.

Disadvantages are:

It may be that programmed materials will increase conformity and reduce creativity. We do not now know.

Some children become bored after short periods of work.

We need to know much more about the relation between pupil interest, attention span, personality characteristics, and successful completion of programs.

We know very little about the amount of time that can profitably be used with programmed materials.

Programmed learning is no better than the program, nor are teaching machines any better than the program in the machine. The only way to evaluate a program is to try it and find out if it produces the desired changes of behavior in children.

The best way to become familiar with programmed learning and teaching machines is to work through a program in a subject new to you. If you have an opportunity, observe pupils using programmed texts in the library and various types of machines in your visual aid department. The proper use of programmed materials requires reappraisal of the daily schedule of the teacher and how he most effectively uses his time.

OTHER RESOURCES FOR LEARNING

Other important resources include flat pictures, posters and charts, maps and globes, models and specimens, chalkboard, field trips and school camping. While these resources are not technological innovations they can enrich learning in the classroom.

Entire books have been written on certain of these resources such as school camping and maps and globes. School camping is on the increase and provides for certain learnings otherwise not obtained. If possible, as part of the reader's teacher training program, he should accompany an elementary class on a camping trip.

There are primarily two types of school camps—the day camp and a camping experience that may extend up to one week. Both types primarily have the same two purposes. The first purpose is to enrich academic subjects through actual experience in the out-of-doors. Many of the opportunities in science education are obvious. There are also excellent opportunities in mathematics, social studies, and language arts. The second purpose is that of providing opportunities for practicing democratic living. Camping can do this in a way that is impossible to do in the schoolroom or on the playground.

In which of these resources are you especially interested? In which do you have special competencies? In which do you wish to develop further competencies? Which have you observed in use in the classroom?

SUMMARY

Skillful manipulation of technologically sophisticated teaching aids must not be confused with the broader significance of skillful selection of the appropriate technique for specific objectives. By themselves, without the concern of the teacher to motivate the learning of the child, audio-visual aids are gadgetry which may merely substitute activity for genuine accomplishment. The long deprived, intensely motivated pupils in underdeveloped countries may be doing a more significant job of learning as they write the dictation of the teacher in their copybooks.

Interaction between teachers and children remains the nucleus of the educational process. It is enhanced, extended, and enriched, but not replaced by TV sets, a multiplicity of devices for use of film, recordings, science charts, tape recorders, and programmed teaching machines. No successful man as yet has attributed his rise in the world to the opaque projector.

SUGGESTED READINGS

Boutwell, William D. (ed.), *Using Mass Media in the Schools*, Appleton-Century-Crofts, New York, 1962.

All forms of mass media are considered. Evaluation of motion pictures, comic books, radio, and television is discussed in the appendix.

Erickson, Carlton W. H., *Fundamentals of Teaching with Audiovisual Technology*. The Macmillan Company, New York, 1965.

Stresses the relationship of the major technological media to productive learning activities. Provides the teacher with a framework for the selection and use of audio-visual materials.

Gerard, Ralph W. ed., *Computers and Education*, McGraw-Hill Book Company, New York, 1967, pp. 11–110.

Deals with computer assisted instruction.

Goodlad, John I. (ed.), *The Changing American School*, 65th Yearbook of the National Society for the Study of Education, Part II, University of Chicago Press, Chicago, 1966.

Chapter IV, written by Edgar Dale, deals with the development, organization, and use of instructional resources.

Kemp, Jerrold E., *Planning and Producing Audiovisual Materials*, Chandler Publishing Company, San Francisco, 1963.

An excellent reference for making your own instructional aids. Photography, graphics, pictures, filmstrips, transparencies, and other aids are included.

Miles, Matthew B. (ed.), *Innovation in Education*, Teachers College, Columbia University, New York, 1964.

Chapters on programmed learning, use of motion pictures, mass media, and other similar methods.

Schultz, Morton J., *The Teacher and Overhead Projection*, Prentice-Hall, Inc., Englewood Cliffs, 1965.

Literally, a treasury of ideas, uses, and techniques of working with the overhead projector. Shows how to make materials to use with the projector. Its use in various subject areas is discussed.

Shores, Louis, *Instructional Materials: An Introduction for Teachers*, The Ronald Press Company, New York, 1960.

Printed materials, graphic materials, motion pictures, recordings, radio and television—all are explored from the standpoint of their uses in education.

The Center for Programmed Instruction, Inc., *A Guide to Programmed Instructional Materials*, Information Division, Center for Programmed Instruction, Inc., Washington, D.C., 1962.

Lists programs available for use, where to get them, and what they cost.

Williams, Catherine M., *Learning From Pictures*, Department of Audiovisual Instruction, National Education Association, Washington, D.C., 1963.

Choosing and using pictures, pictures for subject areas, producing your own pictures, and other helpful suggestions are included. Source lists for pictures are listed in the back of the book.

9

Controversy—
A Continuing Facet
of Education

Controversy is always with us in education. Issues are sometimes extremely important, i.e., those involving the basic purposes of education, and at other times almost petty, i.e., those involving a long-winded controversy over a minor method. The antagonists may be layman vs. layman, professional vs. professional. As with all arguments some are based on reason and others on emotion, bias, and vested interest.

It is important for the beginning student of education to begin to develop an understanding of the areas of controversy and to add continually to his fund of accurate information on the issues.

Some issues result from a basic philosophical or value difference, some from misunderstanding or lack of information. When an individual is fully informed, he can analyze and illuminate the discussion much more effectively than can the superficial or uninformed individual. Too many teachers lack a sound basis for considering the important issues in their profession.

What are the important issues? The list of any two educators would differ. We have discussed some of the issues in the previous chapters. How should we educate the gifted and creative child? What can be done for the culturally different child? How should we organize the elementary school for most effective learning? Is teaching a profession (Chapter 10)? What should we teach in the elementary school? Can we improve the teaching-learning process?

As the reader examines issues, it is important to consider what kinds of issues debate can help clarify and resolve. Which questions listed in the previous paragraph should be settled by discussion between parents and teachers, or by teachers in professional sessions, or by further research? Such highly complex questions as "How can we educate the gifted and culturally different?" and "How can we best organize the elementary school and improve the learning process?" obviously need further research to determine the best answers.

The issue is clearly stated by an expert in human relations, Kenneth D. Benne:

Teachers and parents must always make clear whether they are actually discussing matters of *value* rather than *fact*.[1]

As the reader reads in the area of controversy, he should try to determine whether the issues are ones of *value* or *fact*.

A volume of readings entitled *Crucial Issues in Education*[2] grouped the selections under the major headings of "Censorship, Loyalty and Academic Freedom, Morals and Education, Desegregation in Public Education, Liberal Education for a Scientific Age, Schooling for the Gifted, and New Perspectives for the Teaching Profession." Philip H. Phenix of Teachers College, Columbia University listed twelve areas with a series of questions under each area as follows: curriculum; teaching methods; classification; extra-curricular life; school finance; policy making; teaching as a profession; communism; internationalism; economics; segregation; and religion.[3]

The issues selected for discussion in this chapter deal with

[1]Kenneth D. Benne, "The Debatable in Education," *Childhood Education*, Vol. 41 (April, 1965), p. 400.
[2]Henry Ehlers and Gordon C. Lee, *Crucial Issues in Education*, 3rd ed. (Holt, Rinehart & Winston, Inc., New York, 1964).
[3]Philip H. Phenix, "How to Analyze and Evaluate Educational Controversies," *Arizona Teacher* (March, 1962), pp. 20–21, 29.

attacks on the schools including the freedom to teach, desegregation, the place of religion in the schools, federal aid to education, teacher certification, and the National Education Association vs. the American Federation of Teachers. The discussions presented merely open up the issues for your further exploration. There may be many other issues for a class to explore or there may be certain issues current in the mass media which are challenging.

ATTACKS ON THE SCHOOL

There have always been criticisms of the schools. One for instance: "Not more than half of the boys and girls attending public schools between the ages of 12 and 16 know the names of our Presidents!" That was in the year 1847. Another: "It is a common complaint among business men that young people seeking employment are not well grounded in the fundamentals." (1910)

While criticism of the schools will always be with us, it is extremely important for all citizens to be aware of the nature and sources of such attacks; particularly is this so of the prospective teacher. The problem will probably be especially acute in the years immediately ahead. The editorial section of the St. Louis Post-Dispatch on Tuesday, September 1, 1964, carried this article:

SHARP ATTACK BY EXTREME RIGHT
ON FREEDOM OF EDUCATION IN U.S.
REPORTS TO NEA REVEAL TACTICS SUCH AS
THOSE IN TOTALITARIAN STATES
By Marquis W. Childs

Speaking of conventions and extremists, the Republicans and the Democrats could have learned a lot from educators who met in Seattle before the national parties convened.

As a new school year begins, the evidence presented at the National Education Association deserves re-examination. It shows that at the level of boards of education, PTAs and classrooms, freedom of education and the right of free inquiry are under savage attack.

The record is one of fear and suspicion spread by tactics resembling those of totalitarian states. Extremism at the high school level is not, as a number of speakers related, a theory. It is a practice that has bitten deeply into community after community.

W. R. Fulton, professor of education at the University of Oklahoma, told the NEA convention that irresponsible extremists were "unwilling to accept the legitimacy of debate."

"They often accuse those who oppose their views of being traitors. Such groups are not unlike the extreme left in that they both present a serious threat to individual freedom and the freedom and promise of an open society, both of which are fundamental tenets of PTA."

One of the strongest statements came from Mrs. Jennelle Moorhead of Eugene, Ore., president of the National Congress of Parent Teachers Associations. She described how extremist groups—minority groups—infiltrate PTAs in the drive to take them over. The larger goal is to dominate the school system and dictate what will be taught and who is to teach it, she told teachers from various parts of the country.

"Extremism ignores the real problems of the school—understaffing and underfinancing, the population explosion, the knowledge explosion, the education of the disadvantaged. Instead, it raises ghosts of its own creation, shadows of its own imagining. With jarring repetition it accuses the public schools of not doing the patriotic job they ought to do. It shakes public confidence in teachers, in school administrators and in the PTAs that are the school's staunch allies. Ghosts are no less frightening because they are not real. Extremism rides into power on the waves of fear and confusion it creates."

In "Letters to the Editor" in the September 14, 1964, issue of the Post Dispatch appeared this article:

LETTERS FROM THE PEOPLE

Disease in the PTA

I was greatly alarmed while reading Marquis Childs's article describing the attack of the extreme right on the freedom of education, because I have found similar symptoms in my PTA.

At the opening meeting we had a speaker opposing federal aid to education, after which a vote was taken putting our school on record in opposition to this proposal. When asked why the other side was not presented, the excuse given was "not enough time."

At the next meeting a leader of the local John Birch Society was the speaker. He spoke vehemently about the communistic Supreme Court, our socialistic Federal Government, and proceeded to tear the United Nations to shreds. I couldn't believe this was happening in the school in which my children were learning about our free and democratic society. In the discussion period which followed, the college student exchange program was thoroughly condemned—"letting foreigners go to a school when my child can't get in."

I was further appalled to find the principal and most of the teachers either apathetic or in agreement. There were only a few parents as upset as I who bothered to protest.

I'm confused, distressed and very, very sad.

M.H.

These two articles have been quoted at length for they give an indication that a *third wave* of criticism is upon us. It is apparent that this *third wave* battle will be waged at the "grass roots," and no community knows where it will strike next.

The *first wave* was generally an attack on the patriotism of the schools, teachers, and textbooks. The *second wave* was an attack on the "intellectualism" of the schools, its curriculum, and its teachers. These two waves have been analyzed in a fascinating, if disquieting, volume, *The Ax Grinders*, by Mary Anne Raywid.[4] Broadly speaking the *first wave* was both at individual school level and nationwide occurring between the late 30's and the middle 50's with a definite decrease during World War II. The *second wave* began in the middle 50's and has continued to date. It largely has been debated on the national scene.

It would appear that the *third wave*, supported by extreme

[4]Published by The Macmillan Company, New York, 1962.

rightist views exemplified by the John Birch society, will use the tactics of local infiltration and control by the minority. The twentieth century has supplied many an unforgettable example of how a highly organized minority can take over control.

The Ax Grinders vividly portrays the cooperation between groups attacking education and the complex network of affiliations of the loudest critics. The techniques of the Communists in organizing new groups with basically the same membership is well known. However, the same practice of the extreme right wing group is well documented by Raywid. In addition, the practice of distributing each other's literature is widely followed. Even a few tax exempt "foundations" make their contributions to such groups.

Reduction of taxes is a common theme ranging from proposals to abolish the public schools entirely to the subtle and implied position of the Council on Basic Education that money has nothing to do with good education. Actually, research comparing costs of schools and the quality of programs indicates that money does have considerable to do with good education.

It should be remembered that the stated cause of an attack on the local, state, or national level may be only a smoke screen for the real reason. Once an attack starts, other "chronic complainers" join in for a variety of splenetic reasons. Promptly the original basis spreads, usually supported by literature from the professional "ax grinders."

The possibility that conflicts over schools mirror basic conflicts within society itself is put forth by Raywid.[5] Certainly many of the organizations attacking the schools are against Social Security, public housing, U.N., UNESCO, T.V.A., and civil rights measures, and for drastic reduction of the income tax. It is of course little comfort to the school man to know that the opposition is part of a social, political, economic viewpoint.

What is the answer? There is no simple formula. It is the reader's responsibility as an educated individual and a prospective teacher to be aware of what may happen. The "Letter to

[5] *Ibid.*, p. 198.

the Editor" clearly reflected a school staff either uninformed or apathetic. The best defense is a strong group of concerned citizens in every community who are kept well informed and who support the schools. On the national level the N.E.A. has a Commission for Defense of Democracy, and the National School Public Relations Association is an affiliate. Many state educational associations have a committee or commission comparable to the Commission on Defense of Democracy. A few television programs have helped strengthen the image and the understanding of the problems of teachers. Many newspapers and periodicals are strongly supportive, others are always willing to provide an outlet for the critics.

It is suggested that the reader will find *The Ax Grinders* challenging reading. Also suggested are *Forces Affecting American Education*[6] and *Public Education Under Criticism.*[7] For additional reading on the first wave of criticism, Harold Rugg's book *That Men May Understand*[8] is a fascinating account of the attacks vented upon his social studies textbooks in the late 30's.

INTEGRATION

Segregation was outlawed in our Supreme Court in 1954, and the Civil Rights Act was passed by Congress ten years later in 1964. The struggle for integration goes on both in the north and south. Since the autumn of 1964 there have been more and more southern schools quietly integrating to some extent. A great deal of the thunder during that noisy autumn came from the north with the white boycott at the opening of New York City's schools.

The former U.S. Commissioner of Education, Francis Keppel, stated the case clearly and bluntly:

Let us in the educational family look with boldness and candor at the particulars of civil rights and education,

[6]Association for Supervision and Curriculum Development, 1953 Yearbook (The Association, Washington, D.C., 1953).

[7]C. Winfield Scott and Clyde M. Hill (Prentice-Hall, Inc., Englewood Cliffs, 1954).

[8]Published by Doubleday, Doran and Company, New York, 1941.

of segregation and our schools—the schools which are administered and in which we teach in the name of American democracy.

At the outset, let us be clear about segregation.

Whether it be blatant in the South or subtle in the North, it saps and diminishes democracy and justice. Whether it exists by law or by custom, by edict or by tradition, by patterns of unemployment or patterns of housing, segregation hurts all children, Negro and white alike.

Nowhere is this damage more devastating than in education for democracy.

Therefore I say that the war against segregation is education's war, that it is a single war, but that all too often it is waged on flanks which are secondary to our objective: the elimination of racial discrimination in our schools.

Segregation in our schools was outlawed in its blatant forms in 1954 by the decision of the Supreme Court. But in its subtler forms it calls upon us in education for decision and commitment, for the wisdom to detect the spurious issues from the genuine, the flanking skirmishes from the fundamental struggle.

Today, these flanking forays are taking place in curious sectors—over neighborhood schools, over mobile classrooms, over compensatory education, and even over the use of a school bus.

These secondary issues confuse and divide and frustrate. They lead citizens of good will, teachers of good will, to take passionate stands on one side or the other—and to forget what the enemy is and where the enemy stands.

Through the shortsightedness of many and the recklessness of some, good and allied policies of education are now being turned one against another, bringing the cause of integration into a collision course with the quality of education.[9]

He points out that we need to provide nursery schools for three and four year old culturally different children, enrich their horizons, extend the school day and year, make parents

---

[9]Francis Keppel, "In the Battle for Desegregation—What are the Flanking Skirmishes? What is the Fundamental Struggle?" *Phi Delta Kappan*, Vol. 44 (September, 1964), p. 3.

our partners, ally ourselves with other community agencies, and create a corps of understanding teachers for these schools.

Progress has been slow but steadily discernible. Where deep-rooted, fiercely defensive attitudes are held, change does not come easily.

THE PLACE OF RELIGION IN THE PUBLIC SCHOOLS

The Supreme Court decision in 1962 banning the prescribed prayer of the schools of New York State opened up again the controversy concerning the place of religion in the schools. The accusations, pro and con, flew thick and fast, often hurled most vehemently by people who had not read the actual text of the decision. Undoubtedly more than one pastor immediately opposed the decision from the pulpit only to find later that the official position of the national governing board of his denomination was in favor of the decision. This decision was by no means the beginning of the problem nor will it be the end.

A more detailed examination of the case of Engel versus Vitale will indicate the type of information needed before attempting to draw conclusions. The facts are:

1. The New York State Board of Regents recommended that the following prayer be said each morning:
   "Almighty God, we acknowledge our dependence upon Thee, and we beg Thy blessings upon us, our parents, our teachers and our country."
2. The Board of Education of New Hyde Park, a Long Island community, directed that the prayer be said each morning.
3. Parents of ten pupils brought suit in the New York courts to bar the procedure as obnoxious to their beliefs, religions or religious practices.
4. The New York State Trial Court and the highest court in the state held that there was no constitutional objection as long as no pupil whose parent objected was compelled to join in the prayer.
5. The Supreme Court of the United States in June 1962

reversed the lower courts with five justices joining in the majority decision, Justice Douglas concurred, using a different line of reasoning, and Justice Stewart dissented.

The heart of the majority opinion is the following paragraph:

The petitioners contend among other things that the state laws requiring or permitting use of the Regents' prayer must be struck down as a violation of the Establishment Clause because that prayer was composed by governmental officials as part of a governmental program to further religious beliefs. For this reason, petitioners argue, the State's use of the Regents' prayer in its public school system breaches the constitutional wall of separation between church and state. We agree with that contention since we think that the constitutional prohibition against laws respecting an establishment of religion must at least mean that in this country it is no part of the business of government to compose official prayers for any group of the American people to recite as part of a religious program carried on by government.

The opinion discussed at some length the significance of the First Amendment including the following:

These men knew that the First Amendment, which tried to put an end to governmental control of religion and of prayer, was not written to destroy either. They knew rather that it was written to quiet well-justified fears which nearly all of them felt arising out of an awareness that governments of the past had shackled men's tongues to make them speak only the religious thoughts that government wanted them to speak and to pray only to the God that government wanted them to pray to. It is neither sacrilegious nor antireligious to say that each separate government in this country should stay out of the business of writing or sanctioning official prayers and leave that purely religious function to the people themselves and to those the people choose to look to for religious guidance.

At the end of the last passage the following footnote appears:

There is of course nothing in the decision reached here that is inconsistent, with the fact that school children and others are officially encouraged to express love for our country by reciting historical documents such as the Declaration of Independence which contain references to the Deity or by singing officially espoused anthems which include the composers' profession of faith in a Supreme Being, or with the fact that there are many manifestations in our public life of belief in God. Such patriotic or ceremonial occasions bear no true resemblance to the unquestioned religious exercise that the State of New York has sponsored in this instance.

In his dissenting opinion Justice Stewart states:

I cannot see how an 'official religion' is established by letting those who want to say a prayer say it. On the contrary, I think that to deny the wish of these school children to join in reciting this prayer is to deny them the opportunity of sharing in the spiritual heritage of the Nation.[10]

It is highly important in such a controversy that the well informed individual read the original opinions and not accept unthinkingly the interpretation of columnists and commentators.

In 1963 the Supreme Court ruled that requirements by the state of Maryland for religious exercises, Bible reading, and recitation of the Lord's Prayer were unconstitutional. In previous decisions tax funds have been approved for textbooks (1930 Louisiana) and bus transportation (1947 New Jersey) for parochial and private school children. Released time has been approved (1953 New York) but not when religious instruction is given in the school building (1948 Illinois).

Outside the high court, the public, the Congress, and the state legislatures continue to keep alive the arguments concerning the use of public funds to support religious schools and the place of religion in our schools. Much has been written and will continue to be written on these questions.

[10]For a further discussion of this problem see Sam Duker, "The Supreme Court Ruling on School Prayer," *Educational Forum*, Vol. 27, Part I (November, 1962), pp. 71–77.

In answer to the prayer decision it is significant to recall an answer to a reporter's question by the late President Kennedy in his news conference of June 27, 1962.

> In addition, we have in this case a very easy remedy, and that is to pray ourselves. And I would think that it would be a welcome reminder to every American family that we can pray a good deal more at home, we can attend our churches with a good deal more fidelity, and we can make the true meaning of prayer more important in the lives of all our children. That power is very much open to us. And I would hope that, as a result of this decision, all American parents will intensify their efforts at home. And the rest of us will support the Constitution and the responsibilities of the Supreme Court in interpreting it, which is theirs and given to them by the Supreme Court, by the Constitution.

FEDERAL AID TO EDUCATION

The arguments for and against federal aid to elementary and secondary schools have been heard in numerous sessions of the Congress, in committees responsible for formulating party platforms every four years, in state legislatures, and in the mass media. "Federal Aid means federal control," "Schools are a responsibility of the state and local governments," "Educational opportunities should not depend upon place of residence," and "Many areas cannot afford to finance good schools," echo and re-echo.

A brief look at the historical picture is in order before examining the pros and cons of the argument. Education has largely become a state function and local control is delegated by the respective Constitutions and state legislatures. The decision for the states to exercise primary responsibility for education did not exclude all federal participation. The Continental Congress in 1785 and 1787 provided that the sixteenth section of public lands be devoted to the public schools. The Morrill Act of 1862 laid the foundation for land grant colleges and universities. Since that time various acts have made federal contributions to vocational education, special education, education of Indians, school districts affected by federal activities, the G.I. Bill, school lunches, the National Defense Education

Act of 1958 furnishing assistance to a wide variety of educational programs on all levels, and the extremely comprehensive Elementary and Secondary Education Act of 1965.

In general, such funds have been channelled through the states and there has been relatively little federal control or supervision. Thus, practice has shown the feasibility of federal aid without control. It should be noted, however, that when federal funds are earmarked for special functions they may cause an imbalance. This was one of the criticisms when the National Defense Education Act supplied assistance to foreign language, mathematics, and science programs. Schools emphasized these favored areas during this period rather than others such as social studies, art, and music.

Some of the major arguments in regard to federal aid, pro and con are:

Pro

1. No community lives unto itself alone. Increased mobility necessitates good schools in all areas of the country.
2. Many states and local communities cannot finance adequate programs of education.
3. Adequate educational programs are a necessity for our national defense. Draft rejections for educational deficiencies showed marked differences between states.
4. A program of federal aid can help lessen the marked differences between states and localities.
5. Federal assistance is needed for school construction, teacher salaries and operation.

Con

1. Federal aid will mean federal control.
2. Federal aid will discourage state and local initiative and self-determination.
3. Unless there is federal control, backward communities would use federal funds to lessen tax burdens rather than to improve schools.
4. States can adequately provide for education.
5. Tax reform on a federal, state, and local level could provide adequate funds from state and local sources.
6. A portion of federal aid in some form might go to church supported schools (as recently it has).

The list of arguments can be expanded. Since the federal government is already providing aid in a number of areas, the basic question seems to be "How much and for what purposes?"

The pros and cons of federal aid to education have become somewhat academic with the passage of the Elementary and Secondary Education Act of 1965 (Public Law 89-10). During the first year of the Act there was available a total of $1,300,-000,000 to be distributed under five titles. Title 1 is to improve the educational programs of schools serving a concentration of children from low income families. There was an amount of $1,060,000,000 available under this title. Title 2 was to appropriate money to improve school libraries' sources, textbooks, and other instructional materials. A hundred million was appropriated for this purpose for the first year. Title 3 was to support supplementary educational sources and services. The amount available under this title was $100,000,000. Title 4 was to improve educational research and training, and the sum of a hundred million was appropriated. Title 5 appropriated $25,000,000 to strengthen the state departments of education.

Every precaution was taken to avoid federal control and yet assure that the money went for the purposes intended. The U.S. Office of Education set up certain guidelines in Title 1 and 2 for the states to follow. The states were then primarily responsible for administering the funds allocated to them following the guidelines. Each school system entitled to Title 1 or Title 2 funds had to make application to its State Departments outlining in detail the project or projects for which the funds were to be used. These projects were then approved or disapproved at the state department level.

Applications for monies under Title 3, 4, and 5 were submitted to the U.S. Office of Education, in some cases via the State Departments of Public Instruction. These proposals were carefully evaluated by the U.S. Office of Education staff with the assistance of the recommendations of the specific State Department and utilized the opinions of consultants knowledgeable in the area of the proposal.

There is no question that such allocations of funds to

special programs have a tremendous effect on the programs. Title 1 of Public Law 89-10 is an outstanding example of school systems all over the United States which have children from homes of low incomes that did more in the year 1965–1967 to improve the educational opportunity of these children than had been done in the previous decade. As school systems develop newer ideas and approaches for better educating the children of low income families, we should see a tremendous difference in the achievement and success of these children. The Public Law 89-10 provides an excellent illustration of how federal aid can be utilized to strengthen weak spots and to develop innovative educational programs.

A more comprehensive discussion of the problem is available in V. T. Thayer's *The Role of School in American Society*.[11] Recent articles on the controversy can be found by looking in *The Education Index* under the heading "Federal Aid to Education."

TEACHER CERTIFICATION

It has long been the practice for each state department of education or public instruction to certify individuals who can teach in the state. This practice is followed by states in approving doctors and lawyers. Recently, however, it has been questioned in regard to teachers. The basic assumption involved is that it assures the public of at least a minimum degree of teacher competency.

This minimum degree of competency is extremely important in the case of teachers, as parents have little choice in selecting their child's teacher. If you do not like your doctor, you can change. In most cases, if a parent does not like the child's teacher, the only way to change would be to move to another neighborhood.

In some states a great deal of certification is written into the law by the state legislature. In such cases the provisions are difficult to change and often reflect political opinion rather than the best considered professional opinion. The plan which

[11]Published by Dodd, Mead & Company, New York, 1960, Chapter 24.

both protects the public and utilizes the best professional opinion involves approval of requirements by a lay state board of education based upon recommendations of the best available professional counsel. Such an arrangement would utilize an advisory Teacher Education Committee which would include representatives of teachers, administrators and the teacher-education institutions.

The national trend seems to be for states to define broadly the competencies needed for a teacher, supervisor, and administrator. Each teacher-training institution in the state develops a program for meeting these competencies. Thus programs may use different routes to arrive at the same objectives. These programs are then approved or changes are recommended by the certifying authority. A graduate from such programs is issued a certificate upon the recommendation of his institution. Such a procedure places upon each teacher training institution the *responsibility* of admission, continued evaluation of progress, and final recommendation of each candidate. Such a plan more readily prevents emotionally maladjusted individuals from entering the profession.

Critics of such procedure claim that the control of certification is in the hands of "educationists" and that they perpetuate education courses. This is obviously untrue if the membership of the Teacher Education Committees is well balanced.

The most recent controversy has arisen as a result of a recommendation by James Conant in *The Education of American Teachers*.[12] He recommends that a candidate hold a degree from a legitimate college or university, that the institution determines whether the person is adequately prepared to teach in a designated field and grade level, and that the candidate must be successful as a student teacher in a state department-approved program of student teaching. This proposal would enable an institution to develop any kind of teacher-education program it desired with the exception of student teaching.

Needless to say, such a proposal has brought forth reac-

[12]James Bryant Conant, *The Education of American Teachers* (McGraw-Hill Book Company, New York, 1963).

tions varying from analytical to violent. One vigorous reaction is that of Allen F. Rosebrock of the New Jersey State Department of Education:

> The proposal to place the approval of teacher education programs and standards for teacher licensure within the power of the faculties of the 1,200 individual colleges and universities that prepare teachers amounts to a recommendation of irresponsibility in the most literal sense of the word. Authority over the entire academic and professional program with the exception of student teaching, would be placed in the hands of groups which are not held responsible for the operation of the public schools or accountable for their successes or failures.[13]

Rosebrock goes on to point out that standards are where they belong, "squarely on the shoulders of the lay and professional groups most directly responsible for the conduct of the schools." Not only are the colleges and universities not responsible for public education but many of their faculties have at best only a very superficial knowledge of the problems of the public schools.

What kind of organization exists in your state for certifying teachers? In investigating this question now of so much importance to you, here are related questions which will need to be answered:

> To what extent does your state legislature set requirements?
>
> If you have a lay State Board of Education, is there an advisory Teacher Education or Certification Committee making recommendations to the Board? What kinds of professional people are on the Committee?
>
> To what extent can your own college or university determine the program of teacher education, and to what extent is it determined on the state level?

[13]Allen F. Rosebrock, "A Symposium on James Bryant Conant's *The Education of American Teachers*," *Journal of Teacher Education*, Vol. 15 (March, 1964), pp. 17–18.

Does your institution recommend graduates for certification or can you apply directly to the state department?[14]

NATIONAL EDUCATION ASSOCIATION VS.
AMERICAN FEDERATION OF TEACHERS

The fall of 1961 marked the beginning of intensified rivalry between the two major organizations for teachers, the National Education Association (NEA) and the American Federation of Teachers (AFT). New York City teachers had to select an agent to bargain with the Board of Education. The contest was between the United Federation of Teachers, an affiliate of the American Federation of Teachers, connected with the AFL-CIO, and the Teachers Bargaining Organization, supported by the National Education Association. The UFT won. Since then the practice of "professional negotiations" between teachers organizations and Boards of Education has rapidly spread. By the spring of 1968 the NEA local groups had been selected as negotiating agent in more cities, while the AFT was the representative for more teachers. The AFT was thus more successful in being selected as negotiating agent for certain very large cities.

The National Education Association was first organized as the National Teachers Association in 1857 and became the National Education Association in 1870. The policies of the NEA are decided by over 5,000 delegates for affiliated state and local organizations meeting in annual conventions early each summer. In the spring of 1968 its membership was over 1,081,800.

The American Federation of Teachers, an affiliate of the AFL-CIO, was organized in 1916 and at the beginning of 1968 had a membership over 144,500. The governing body is the annual convention which is composed of elected representatives from the locals.

One primary difference is that superintendents of schools

[14]If you wish to read further in this field start with the March, 1964, issue of *The Journal of Teacher Education*, follow with James B. Conant's book. A stimulating volume in this area is Sam P. Wiggin's *Battlefields in Teacher Education* (George Peabody College for Teachers, Nashville, 1964).

cannot hold membership in the AFT. They are considered to be responsible to the Board of Education. A few years ago the positions of organized labor and the AFT seemed to coincide. Recently, however, labor has begun to oppose certain taxes that would benefit the schools. What constitutes a "fair" tax proposal is always a controversy.

One of the arguments of the NEA is that teachers should represent the best interests of all the children of all the people. To affiliate with one segment of society weakens their position. The AFT replies that the only way teachers can attain their rights is to affiliate with labor. The arguments show no signs of abatement. One thing seems to be clear. The NEA is becoming much more militant in promoting "professional negotiations" backed by "sanctions" and the AFT, while not lessening its militancy, is becoming more concerned with professional problems. Teacher strikes, led by one group or the other, are markedly on the increase.

A united profession does not impose bland unanimity upon its members; however, differences should not become so divisive that the profession is weakened in the face of irresponsible attacks.

SUMMARY

What were the educational beliefs you held at the beginning of this course? Which ones have changed? What experiences were responsible for changing them? As you gradually become a teacher you will be strengthening some beliefs, developing new convictions and discarding others. It is important that your attitudes and beliefs be strongly based upon facts and understanding rather than upon unexamined emotional responses.

Educational controversy will exist throughout your career as a teacher. The issues will differ. You will be a participant in the discussion of such issues in the teacher's room, in faculty meetings, around the bridge table, in casual conversations and in public meetings, and through your membership in professional associations.

Agnes Snyder, who has spent a lifetime working for the improvement of early childhood education, advises:

It is particularly important that we who teach find our credo, our credo of education, our credo of life. For we are what we believe and we do as we are, and these exert a far greater influence on children than anything we may give them by way of precept. So we ask ourselves; Is there anything that is undebatable? If so, what is it for me? And what is debatable—that of which I am not sure? And how can I find the answer for me? There is an answer for you and for me. There are roadways to the answer—arduous, it is true, and infinitely satisfying, not only at the end of the road but all along the way.

There is no one answer. I have purposely repeated, "for me." The essence of the undebatable is conviction, and each must find that for himself.[15]

Continuing, she suggests "roads" to follow to develop our credo:

It is imperative that we be sure; but never so sure, so inflexible, that we become deaf to new voices. Knowing the problems and issues besetting mankind and participating in our own sphere to their solution; gaining perspective through searching the pages of history for the thoughts and deeds of those who have gone before us; being alert to modified and enriched concepts through the findings of research and our own experience; being willing to submit even our most deeply held convictions to responsible debate these are roads that will lead us to sureness.[16]

SUGGESTED READINGS

Association for Supervision and Curriculum Development, *Forces Affecting American Education*, 1953 Yearbook, The Association, Washington, D.C., 1953.

Chapter III deals with groups affecting education.

[15]Agnes Synder, "How Sure Can We Be?" *Childhood Education*, Vol. 41, No. 8 (April, 1965), p. 391. Reprinted by permission of the Association for Childhood Education International, 3615 Wisconsin Ave., N.W., Washington, D.C.

[16]*Ibid.*

"A Symposium on James Bryant Conant's The Education of American Teachers," *Journal of Teacher Education*, Vol. 15, March 1964, Entire volume.

A most significant group of pro and con reactions to Conant's recommendations.

Clift, Virgil A., Archibald W. Anderson, and H. Gordon Hullfish (eds.), *Negro Education in America*, Harper and Row, Publishers, New York, 1962.

This yearbook of the John Dewey Society provides a comprehensive analysis of the problem of Negro education. Part IV is especially timely in terms of emphasis on improved education for the culturally deprived.

Coleman, James S., "The Coleman Report: Opening Pandora's Box," U.S. Government Printing Office, 1966, 743 pp.

The Civil Rights Act of 1964 directed the Commissioner of Education to survey inequality of educational opportunity among all groups in the U. S. This report has resulted in marked controversy.

Commission on Religion in the Public Schools, *Religion in the Public Schools*, American Association of School Administrators, Washington, D.C., 1964.

An authoritative statement on the place of religion in the schools. Valuable chapters on the law and ways schools can accommodate to religious pluralism including suggestions for Christmas celebrations.

Conant, James Bryant, *The Education of American Teachers*, McGraw-Hill Book Company, New York, 1963.

Based on a survey of a number of teacher-training institutions, Conant makes a series of recommendations. Considerable controversy has arisen over some of those recommendations.

Cremin, Lawrence A., *The Transformation of the School*, Alfred A. Knopf, Inc., New York, 1961.

Modern controversy has its roots in the past. This volume, especially Chapter IX, illuminates the controversy over progressive education.

Ehlers, Henry and Gordon C. Lee, *Crucial Issues in Education*, 3rd ed., Holt, Rinehart & Winston, Inc., New York, 1964.

An excellent collection of readings on various controversies.

Elam, Stanley, Myron Lieberman and Michael H. Moskow, *Read-*

ings on Collective Negotiations in Public Education, Rand, McNally, Chicago, 1967.

This book of 40 readings is basic in obtaining some insight into one of the most recent "hot" issues in education.

Frommer, Arthur (ed.), *The Bible and the Public Schools*, The Frommer-Pasmantier Publishing Corporation, New York, 1963.

A detailed account of the Supreme Court's decision of June 17, 1963 dealing with devotional Bible reading in the public schools, background and complete text of the decision. Contains also the text of the New York prayer decision.

Full, Harold, *Controversy in American Education*, The Macmillan Co., New York, 1967.

An anthology dealing with issues in society, school, youth, the professor and European schools.

Raywid, Mary Anne, *The Ax Grinders*, The Macmillan Company, New York, 1962.

A fascinating account of the groups attacking the public schools, their methods and interrelationships. A must reading.

Rugg, Harold, *That Men May Understand*, Doubleday, Doran and Company, New York, 1941.

A detailed account of attacks on one series of textbooks. Basic to understanding the wider significance of what might appear to be a local attack on a single library or textbook.

"The Politics of Education", *Phi Delta Kappan*, Vol. 49 (February, 1968).

Does an educator need political know-how? This issue provides some challenging answers. The *Phi Delta Kappan* publishes some of the most controversial material found in education magazines.

10

Teaching— a Profession

One of the classic educational arguments was "Is teaching a profession?" It is now recognized as a profession, and the major problem is for all of us to help teaching become more effective and responsible. The effectiveness of any profession depends on each member's willingness to accept the responsibilities, obligations, and challenges of his membership therein.

CHARACTERISTICS OF A PROFESSION

There are several characteristics of a profession. One is that the services of professions are of *critical importance to society*. A member should give priority to the welfare of society. As a result, most professions have developed a code of ethics to govern the behavior of their members. Committees of the National Education Association have evolved over the years the present code of ethics which was adopted by the Association in July, 1963. Each state association also has its own code, usually similar to the NEA code.

The code constitutes a behavior guide for the teacher in his personal life and in his relations with students, parents, the community, the employing board and other teachers. As soon as the teacher begins his training, he has begun to assume professional responsibility. When he enters a classroom to observe, he does so as a professional. When he helps one student, when he participates in September Experience, when he does his student teaching, and when he acquires information concerning a student in connection with a course, he does so as a professional. In all of these dealings his behavior should conform to the code.

A second characteristic of a profession is that it *requires a high level of intellectual competence and professional skills*. Involved is not only a period of foundational training but continuous upgrading while you are practicing your profession. A number of states require five years of training for teachers. Increasingly such five-year programs involve four years of pre-service training followed by some intern experience. The additional year of college can be taken in summers or in a regular session.

Unfortunately, we have not yet reached the stage where only fully qualified people are allowed to teach. If there is a marked shortage of teachers in a state, too often individuals with sub-standard training are accepted. Usually the parents whose children are placed with such a teacher have no idea of his status. We wonder what would happen if a sign were placed outside of the door of each such person which read "Enter at your own risk, this teacher is not fully qualified."

The third characteristic of a profession is the *guarantee to the public that an individual is competent to practice*. This guarantee is in the form of the state's assuming the responsibility of granting a license. In the case of teachers it is called certification. Every teacher must be certified by the state. If a teacher moves to another state, he must be certified in that state. There is considerable variation from state to state in requirements. It is not unusual for a teacher well trained in one state to be required to take one or more courses in moving to another state. For instance, California for years required a course in audio-visual aids.

A teacher-training institution must be accredited to train teachers. This accrediting is being done more and more by the National Council for Accreditation of Teacher Education

(NCATE) with the assistance of representatives from the state certifying agency. Formerly each state usually listed specific courses and specific hours of credit required. Increasingly, institutions are being permitted to develop the best possible program and the state approves this program or suggests changes. Then a graduate from such an approved program is certified by the state. This procedure places the responsibility for recommendation upon the teacher-training institution, and the state does not have to accept a specific pattern of courses appearing on a transcript. When the responsibility is placed upon an institution, factors other than credits can determine whether the student is recommended for certification. A maladjusted student who should not be working with children can be identified by the institution and not recommended for a certificate. The responsibility for the selection of students entering the program, for retention in the program, and final recommendation rests solely with the institution.

A fourth characteristic of a profession is that it is *organized to promote professional activities and growth*. The organization in education with the largest membership is the National Education Association. Each state has a state educational association with which local groups of teachers are affiliated. Then there are many special interest groups on both a national, state, and local or area level. Many of these were listed in Chapter 1 along with their major types of publications.

You may have already begun your membership in the National Education Association by your membership in high school in the Future Teachers of America. Most institutions have a group affiliated with the Student National Education Association and the state educational association. Members receive the *NEA Journal* and the monthly *Student NEA News* and have opportunity to participate in group life insurance.

If you have a chapter on the campus, the quality of the chapter depends on you and your associates. There are many interest groups on campus as there are in every community, vying for your interest. It is important that early in your professional life you balance social activity with professional activity.

There are also professional fraternities which outstanding

undergraduate students are often invited to join. Phi Delta Kappa is for men, Pi Lamda Theta for women, and Kappa Delta Pi for both. These are strong professional organizations with strong programs for improving education. The journal *Phi Delta Kappan* is one of the most lively and significant journals in education. It welcomes controversy to its pages. If ever you are invited to join one of the organizations, you will prize your membership for your entire professional career.

Since the purpose of an overview is expository rather than persuasive, it would be inappropriate to engage in recruitment for a specific professional organization. The ink will scarcely be dry on the teacher's first contract before his colleagues will be advancing the merits of the National Education Association or the American Federation of Teachers. It is hoped that his decision will be made on the basis of issues rather than upon the personalities of the various advocates. It is urged that the teacher join one or the other on national, state, and local levels and be concerned with the program of his choice. The uncommitted loner does not do his share to further advance his profession even though he benefits from the advantages that have already been secured by his committed colleagues.

In addition, if the teacher has a special interest, he should join the appropriate association. For instance, if he is interested in reading, becoming a member of the International Reading Association will bring him its publications including *The Reading Teacher*. Many teachers in the elementary schools are members of a local branch of the Association for Childhood Education and are regular readers of *Childhood Education*.

TEACHERS' SALARIES

During the past ten years certain encouraging trends have occurred in relation to teachers' salaries:

The U.S. average of teachers' salaries increased faster than wage and salary levels in the whole economy.

Average salaries of teachers increased faster than the cost of living and faster than the wage gains of all workers combined.

We still face the fact that:

Despite all the gains, teachers' salaries in 1960 were far below the average earnings of other professional workers.[1]

Most school systems have a definite salary schedule which provides additional increments of salary with additional years of experience and additional training. Most districts have single salary schedules, that is elementary teachers receive the same pay as do secondary teachers for the same training and experience. When average salaries are studied, the secondary teachers have a higher average due to higher average training. Some of this differential is due to the additional amounts for special duties, such as coaching, paid by many schools.

Favorable situations in the United States are most encouraging. For the school year 1964–65, 107 school systems of those studied reported minimums for a BA of $5,400, MA maximums of $9,500, and scheduled maximums of $11,000 or more. With the exception of two districts in Alaska, these are suburban areas near Los Angeles, San Francisco, Chicago, and New York City. Such systems not only have the highest salary schedules, but they are most selective of personnel, provide excellent assistance for the teachers in terms of specialized personnel and materials, and have highly qualified administrators. A number of these districts hire beginning teachers who have just completed their training. It is obvious that they can select from "the cream of the crop."

Consider some other facts concerning salaries. Thirty-two of the fifty states have statutory minimum salary requirements. Naturally, school boards in these states can pay more than the minimum.

The average salary paid elementary teachers in 1966–67 was $6,609.

The differences between regions reflect to some extent differences in qualifications of teachers.

These figures, while showing the overall picture, do not

[1]N.E.A. Research Bulletin, Vol. 40 (December, 1962), p. 101. See also Vol. 41, December, 1963, Vol. 42, February, 1964, December, 1964, and Vol. 45, March 1967, for the figures quoted in this section.

reflect some of the basic problems of raising the money. The *NEA Research Bulletin* points out that:

> The general property tax carries 55 per cent of the cost of public education and accounts for almost all support by local governments. But this tax yields only 14.5 per cent of all tax collections and must support over half the cost of our largest and costliest domestic enterprises.
>
> State and local sources of school money cannot match the growth of education; additional support from the federal tax systems seems to be the only answer.[2]

In general, the school districts spending the most to educate each student are the wealthier districts in each state. They have less trouble raising their budgets than do the poorer districts which spend much less per capita. We have a long way to go to achieve "raising the money where the wealth is and educating the children where they are."

The reader would find it a most interesting study to locate some financial data for his state. What is the difference in average salary paid in your state between the district with the lowest average salary and the one with the highest? What is the difference in per capita cost for each student in these districts? What is the difference in taxable wealth per student in these districts? What plan is used in your state for equalizing educational opportunity by providing for state funds for education?

CAREER OPPORTUNITIES

By far the largest group of personnel employed by the school is the classroom teacher. Formerly most college students training to be elementary school teachers felt that they would probably teach in a self-contained classroom in either primary or intermediate grades. Their basic preparation was similar except for emphasizing their chosen level in their observations and student teaching. Now more possibilities are opening up for the college student who specializes in a subject area. Some of the plans for team teaching give teachers an opportunity to

[2]Vol. 41, December, 1963, p. 99.

specialize in one or two subject areas. While this specialization does not require a major in a subject area, as it does for the secondary teacher, it does require some concentration of courses. Often this concentration can be achieved by using the electives available in most programs.

The elementary school librarian is a position which is definitely on the increase. Such an individual should have broad training as an elementary teacher plus specialized library and audio-visual training.

The elementary school counselor is another emerging position. The ideal background for such a position would include training on the pre-service level as an elementary teacher with considerable emphasis on courses in psychology, sociology, and anthropology. Graduate work after some teaching experience should be in the areas of child development, measurement, guidance, and counseling. The individual must also have experience in working with teachers on problems of children.

There is an increase in the use of consultants in the various subject areas. Art and music consultants have been utilized for some time. The demand for reading specialists is increasing. Opportunities for science, mathematics, social studies, language, and physical education specialists are also on the increase. Individuals selected for such positions are usually outstanding teachers who have had graduate work in their area of specialty. Art, music, and physical education teachers need a strong concentration of undergraduate courses in their speciality. The requirements for teachers of the handicapped or the gifted were discussed in Chapter 3.

Each school has a principal who presumably understands the instructional program of the elementary school and can work effectively with teachers. Most states require an administrator's certificate, necessitating graduate work in administration and supervision. A large proportion of elementary school principals are men. Most women who have been appointed to the principalship have had a great deal of teaching experience in addition to their graduate work.

Actually the quickest route for the young person who eventually wishes to become a school administrator is an undergraduate training program in elementary education and teaching experience at various grade levels accompanied by graduate work for the elementary principalship. Such an individual should have better than average grades. Electives on the undergraduate level should be taken in political science, sociology, economics, and psychology. More outstanding men are sorely needed in elementary education, and there is a bright future for the ones willing to work.

Elementary school supervisors are individuals who were outstanding elementary school teachers and did graduate work in supervision. Women generally occupy such positions though not always. Curriculum directors are experienced teachers who have done graduate work in the curriculum area and often have teaching experience on both the elementary and secondary levels. These people must be individuals who can work effectively with teachers. They need to keep informed of curriculum developments in all subjects, kindergarten through grade 12. Superintendents of schools usually have had experience as either elementary or secondary school principals. They are expected to have completed at least two years of graduate work with a major in educational administration.

There is another possibility that few undergraduates in elementary education ever consider and that is becoming a professor of elementary education on the college level. College teaching is expanding and can be a satisfying profession. One can combine teaching, writing, and research to provide an interesting career. A Ph.D. or an Ed.D. is a requirement if you are to receive recognition and promotion. If your scholastic average is high, this may be an area to which you should give careful consideration. Practically all of your instructors have had experience as elementary teachers or administrators, then have obtained their master's degrees, and finally decided to work on their doctorates. We need more students who plan early to work for their doctorates. If the decision is made at the beginning of graduate work, a better program can be developed. The best preparation for a doctoral program would include a strong concentration of courses in one subject area of the elementary school and a good background in the behavioral sciences including psychology, sociology, and anthropology. A year of statistics should be completed by the end of the Master's program. In addition a background in history, philosophy, and psychology of education is needed, as well as thorough training in graduate work in elementary education.

There are many outstanding women undergraduate students who should give consideration to working for a Ph.D., or Ed.D. in elementary education. Women too often postpone the decision, being more interested in Mrs. than Ph.D. Many college women who have earned their teaching credentials return to teaching after their children are in school.

Specialists may be invited to speak before your class so you can become informed of their work. Anyone in the teaching profession is most happy to confer with a prospective teacher about opportunities in his area. You can look up the certification requirements in your state for specialized personnel, and you can explore the possibility of scholarships and fellowships available on both the undergraduate and graduate levels.

IS ELEMENTARY TEACHING THE PROFESSION FOR ME?

This question has been left until now with the hope that you will have a better basis for answering this question than at the beginning of the book. It is hoped that during the quarter or semester the reader has had many experiences which will help him arrive at a more considered answer. These might include opportunities to observe elementary classes, to work with one child, to view instructional materials used in the schools, to view films, to read widely, and to talk with school people. You have had the beginning of a look at elementary education as a teacher sees it, rather than relying upon hazy recall of your experience in the elementary school.

Here a long pious list of qualities needed by elementary teachers could be given, but such a list is discouraging for as ordinary human beings we have our strengths and our shortcomings. Most good elementary teachers are far from being paragons of all the virtues. It is more realistic for you to examine a few basic questions.

Do I enjoy working with children of elementary school

age? If the answer is no, stay away from elementary school teaching. Children know the teachers who enjoy teaching and those who hate it. It can be satisfying, exciting work if you like children. If your answer by now is "I don't know because I haven't had much contact with children," use every opportunity available for such contact. Church groups, Boy Scouts, Girl Scouts, and Campfire Girls are always in need of additional leadership. Get the necessary experience immediately.

Am I as emotionally mature for my age as other college students? In college you are in the process of becoming emotionally mature. What is your pattern of behavior with others? Do you lose your temper easily? Do you use sarcasm often? Do you overreact to criticism? Can you manage your time adequately? Do you assume responsibility for directing yourself? The individual who "flies off the handle" at the least provocation has no place in the classroom, nor has the person who is not self-directive.

If this is your freshman year, you have probably grown more self-directive. Undoubtedly you manage both your time and money better than when you entered college. If you have special problems in the area of emotional adjustment, be sure to utilize the counseling services available in your college.

Do I have the intellectual ability to enter teaching? You need more than the traditional "gentleman's C" point of view. Teachers who keep education in a state of vigorous evolvement need better than average academic competence continuously activated by intellectual curiosity—not for them the hand-me-down answers, the minimum effort, the mimeographed busy work either for their own or for children's education.

Are you satisfied with only doing the minimum for each course or do you occasionally follow interesting leads way beyond the prescribed limits? Do you enjoy intellectual activities? If your grade point average is on the border line, discuss the problem with your advisor. It may be that you have poor study habits or reading difficulties. Most colleges have special programs, classes, or clinics that can help you if you need it.

The initiative to become a good teacher must come from you. There are many things you can do on your own. Your effectiveness in the classroom and as a faculty team member will require that you present yourself as effectively as possible. Begin now to anticipate your role and responsibilities.

A voice which carries pleasantly to the back of the school room is a necessity. A teacher has to feel comfortable in speaking. Unless you have had training in vocal music or dramatic experience in the college theater, you probably need analysis and development of enunciation and resonance. Neither a murmurer nor a shouter can manage an active classroom. Many experienced teachers are appalled to hear tape recordings of their speech. A beginner will be well advised to develop an expertly modulated voice which is both audible to the farthest corners of the classroom and at the same time calming to the children. Specific techniques are involved which are not picked up by trial and error.

A teacher must participate in many activities with his colleagues and other adults. Do you feel comfortable with other students? Do you participate in some of the many groups on a college campus? College furnishes many opportunities for you to feel socially adequate in a wide variety of situations. Do not back away, but on the other hand do not get so involved that your classwork suffers.

The way one views his future courses in elementary education will make a real difference in his effectiveness as a teacher. Indifferent college students who avoid the many available opportunities to work with children and to observe classes will feel that education courses are mostly theory. They will see theory as having little meaning to them as future teachers. Experienced teachers who return for graduate work in education find these courses immediate and profitable, for they see the relationship of the content to the classroom.

It is unavoidably certain that a course in child development isolated from contact with children will seem highly theoretical. When enriched with opportunities to work with children the concepts come alive in the behavior of boys and girls. That "Aggressiveness is one reaction to frustration" is clearly seen in the incident in which disadvantaged Bill caused trouble because the lesson was beyond his understanding. The excitement in the faces of a group of culturally different kindergarten children on a field trip brings meaning to "culturally

deprived children who have had a very limited environment."
Hearing the best and poorest reader in the third grade read
aloud vitalizes that "There is a wide range of reading ability
in the usual classroom." Your own experiences or lack of them
will make the difference in whether or not courses are to go
beyond inanimate verbalization.

SUMMARY

Much of this final chapter has been concerned with the
details of a constantly evolving profession, with standards and
salaries and certification, and with salaries and ethics and
organizations. Emerging opportunities for specialized careers
in elementary education have been described briefly to suggest
long-term plans for one's work.

The heart of the matter, compared to which all other considerations are peripheral, is whether you really wish more
than anything else to be a teacher. It can be both a satisfying
and a frustrating life. Everybody who ever went to school is a
self-appointed expert on the right way to do your job. Sometimes the profession is beleaguered, belittled, and beset by
every loop of the lunatic fringe. Sometimes progress with children seems glacially slow. If one is short of patience as a
beginner, he must search for hidden wellsprings of compassion
within himself before his contribution to children can emerge
unhampered. If one is overly impatient to remold the world
through the classroom, he must curb the insistence of ego and
try to work with colleagues, parents, and other citizens through
the often turtle-torpid processes of group action.

None of the drawbacks which any old hand can point
out can dim the resolve of a determined youngster who wants
to teach, who enjoys children even when they are far from
cherubic, and who wants to follow the honorable calling of
giving as much or more to life than one receives. It is these
who renew and revive the profession every year as they sign
in on their first time sheet and stand bravely against the con-
centrated stare of the third grade as it appraises the new
teacher.

If you know that this is the life for you, welcome. You

are needed by the tens of thousands and more. The children who will be in charge of the twenty-first century deserve the best education you can give.

SUGGESTED READINGS

Ashton-Warner, Sylvia, *Teacher*, Simon and Schuster, Inc., New York, 1963.
   A very interesting summary of twenty-four years of teaching in an elementary school. "Organic" teaching is the theme.

Brembeck, Cole S., *The Discovery of Teaching*, Prentice-Hall, Inc., Englewood Cliffs, 1962.
   Do you really want to teach? Chapters I through V help answer the questions by furnishing descriptions of problems of student teachers and of the classroom.

Grambs, Jean Dresden, *Schools, Scholars, and Society*, Prentice-Hall, Inc., Englewood Cliffs, 1965.
   Chapters XI and XII provide an interesting picture of teachers and their confusions.

Kaufman, Bel, *Up the Down Staircase*, Prentice-Hall, Inc., Englewood Cliffs, 1964.
   The voices and writings of adolescents, the squeak of the administrative machinery, the frustrations and victories of an English teacher in a large metropolitan high school all speak loudly and clearly in these pages.

Kinney, Lucien B., *Certification in Education*, Prentice-Hall, Inc., Englewood Cliffs, 1964.
   A summary of the present situation in teacher certification. Chapter IX discusses the profession's responsibility for quality of its membership.

Ryans, David G., *Characteristics of Teachers: A Research Study*, American Council on Education, Washington, D.C., 1960.
   A careful study of good teachers' characteristics, using observation, statistical techniques, and standardized testing procedures.

Stinnett, T. M. and Huggett, Albert J., *Professional Problems of Teachers*, The Macmillan Company, New York, 1963.
   An extensive discussion of the responsibilities of teachers to the school and the community, including an examination of ways to meet these responsibilities.

INDEX

THE ALLYN AND BACON SERIES
FOUNDATIONS OF EDUCATION

Society, Schools, and Learning
Wilbur B. Brookover and Edsel L. Erickson

Teachers and Learners: The Interactive Process of Education
Alfred H. Gorman

Introduction to Philosophy of Education
James Gribble

Allyn and Bacon, Inc.
470 Atlantic Avenue
Boston, Massachusetts 02210

222412